Everything I Ever Wanted

EVERYTHING I EVER WANTED

The life and career of
Peggy Mount

by
Andrew Ross

fantom
publishing

First published in 2019 by Fantom Publishing, an imprint of Fantom Films
www.fantompublishing.co.uk

A catalogue record for this book is available from the British Library.

Hardback edition ISBN: 978-1-78196-321-0

Typeset by Phil Reynolds Media Services, Leamington Spa
Printed and bound by CPI Group (UK) Ltd, Croydon, CR0 4YY

For Eira and Harry Darton

And
In Loving Memory of
Sandra Newton
"For Valour"

Also by Andrew Ross and published by Fantom

Too Happy A Face
The authorised biography of Joan Sims

Contents

Acknowledgements		ix
Preface		xiii
1	A troubled childhood	1
2	Treading the boards	10
3	*Sailor, Beware!*	36
4	A star is born	57
5	Dragon and beyond	68
6	Theatre legend	100
7	'Dame' Peggy	127
8	Slow curtain…	151
Stage credits		170
Film credits		178
Television credits		181
Radio credits		185
Bibliography		188
Notes on the chapters		190
Index		204

Contents

Acknowledgements

I WOULD LIKE TO THANK the following actors, agents, authors, individuals and agencies for their responses and help:

Dean Barker, Tim Brooke-Taylor, Vivienne Clore, Kaye Crawford, Bernard Cribbins OBE, Clare Eden, Simon Flavin (Mirrorpix), David Goldwater, Deborah Grant, David Hodges (*Radio Times*), Georgy Jamieson, Sue Jennings (PA to Dame Judi Dench), Bo Keller, Catherine Johnson, Anne Lewis, Andy Merriman, Ralph Montagu (*Radio Times*), Callum J. Phoenix, Jeremy Preston, David Simpson (Palace Theatre Club Archives), Paul Stephen.

Special thanks

I am greatly indebted to the following individuals for taking the time to share with me their memories of Peggy Mount, OBE:

Thelma Barlow, Jean Bayliss, Baroness Floella Benjamin OBE, Alan Bennett, Philip & Sally Brazier, Ayshea Brough, Bill Bryden CBE, Judy Buxton, the late Pat Coombs, Ray Cooney OBE, Nick Corrigan, Sir Tom Courtenay, Mark Curry, Niamh Cusack, Harry and Eira (Griffiths) Darton, Freddie Davies, Dame Judi Dench, Zulema Dene, Angela Douglas, Philip Draycott, Nigel Ellacott, Norman Eshley, Jean Fergusson, Patricia Franklin, Terence Frisby, Oliver Ford Davies, Mike Grady, Georgina Hale, Damaris Hayman, Penny Hey, Diana Hoddinott, Jeffrey Holland, John Holmes, Peter Holmes, Sir Derek Jacobi, Louise Jameson, Judy Jarvis, Gareth Jones, Niall Leonard, Mark Lester, Christine Lohr, Harry & Joan Maggs, Lindsay Maggs, Ian Masters, Claudia Mayer, Sylvester McCoy, Sir Ian McKellen, Georgina Moon, Mark Piper, Penny Ryder, Ann Sidney, Howard Schuman, David Scott, Jack Smethurst, John Standing, Tommy Steele OBE, Pam Valentine, Johnny Wade, Duncan C. Weldon (1941-2019), Dame Penelope Wilton, Dame Barbara Windsor MBE.

I am especially indebted to Peggy's dear friends, Eira and Harry Darton, for their involvement in this project and for their friendship, hospitality and invaluable memories of their friend. When I first contacted them regarding the possibility of writing a book on their famous friend, Eira responded by writing 'such a venture would indeed be a very long overdue recognition of someone who brought an immense creative presence to any stage, TV and film project'. I am so pleased that they have both been happy to share their memories of 'Peg' for others to enjoy.

I would also like to thank my parents for their love and encouragement, Jeffrey Holland and Judy Buxton for their help and valued friendship and the late Fenella Fielding OBE for her much-cherished friendship and interest in my work.

Finally my late friend and pen-pal, actress Pat Coombs, gave great insight into Peggy's final days and their interesting friendship and ultimately provided the inspiration for this book.

Peggy Mount as the Nurse in Zeffirelli's *Romeo and Juliet*
(Drawing by Victoria Johnson, reproduced with permission)

Preface

FROM 1997 UNTIL HER DEATH in May 2002 I was friends and pen-pals with the late, much-loved actress, Pat Coombs. It was via 'Patty' that I became familiar with Peggy Mount – the leading actress of stage, screen and television – with whom Patty had worked on television during the 1970s and early 1980s. The pair had been friends for years and when Peggy became a resident at Denville Hall, the exclusive actors' retirement home in Northwood, Patty was one of her most regular visitors.

Patty's letters and notes were always welcome and filled with titbits on her day-to-day activities, health issues and of course theatrical news. Increasingly as her visits to Denville became more frequent, so too did her references to Peggy Mount. Although at the time I was relatively unfamiliar with Peggy's work, I quickly learned about the remarkable lady with whom I shared a mutual friend. It was always a source of interest and sometimes amusement to hear, via Patty, of

Peggy's antics and occasional outbursts. It was clear from Patty's letters, filled with multiple exclamation marks and underlined words, that Peggy was a strong and sometimes difficult character – clearly a force to be reckoned with.

Eventually, having built up a good idea of what life was like at Denville Hall from her regular visits, Patty decided to become a permanent resident there herself and in doing so became even closer to Peggy. In many ways this was ironic since the two ladies had played a pair of friends living in a retirement home in the Yorkshire Television sitcom *You're Only Young Twice*. The similarities of life imitating art were not lost on many of those who were friends with the two actresses.

Peggy Mount died at Denville Hall on 13th November 2001, following a period of declining health. Six months later, on 25th May 2002, Pat Coombs also died at Denville following a prolonged and brave battle with osteoporosis, emphysema and gangrene of the legs.

In many ways it was a mixed blessing that the two friends died within a short space of time. Although their relationship had its ups and down, as most friendships generally do, it is clear that their final days were spent in comfort – indeed Denville Hall is often compared to a five-star hotel. It is touching that the two ladies, neither of whom had married or had children, were able to spend the final phase of their lives in close proximity.

Patty's letters provided the inspiration for this biography of Peggy's long life and prestigious career. In researching this book it has been evident that Peggy Mount was in many ways a pioneer; an actress who, although typecast in some ways, was able to enjoy a diverse career in every area and every genre of acting – from light-hearted theatrical farce to thought-provoking television drama. Although forever remembered as the booming-voiced 'battleaxe' of British entertainment, Peggy Mount was much more than a 'dragon'. She became a star in the West End at the age of forty and remained a star actress for the next forty years as she worked her way through dozens of plays as well as starring roles in films and countless appearances on television and radio.

Despite decades in the public eye, Peggy remained a very private person. Other than to promote her latest appearance on stage she rarely gave interviews and was always reluctant to discuss her private life. Indeed few journalists were brave enough to delve into her past or ask questions on personal matters. Peggy Mount was never interested in the idea of 'celebrity'. She was a professional actress who cherished her work and her privacy in equal measure. Her small circle of trusted friends, built up over many years, was very dear to her but carefully chosen.

Towards the end of her life Peggy donated some items of memorabilia to a charity auction in aid of the Ken Hill Musical Theatre Trust. When she decided to move into Denville Hall she was 'ruthless' in clearing out or destroying such items relating to her life and career. As a result, virtually no personal record of Peggy's life was left behind. She remained proud of her OBE insignia and certificate, and certain items of porcelain, glass and pictures remained in her collection, but generally speaking – and to the horror of any biographer or researcher – she did not preserve any photographs, letters or diaries. In compiling this account of her life and career, I have therefore been reliant on those who knew her best to share their memories and on secondary sources. I hope their thoughts and memories help provide a rounded picture of this remarkable lady.

Andrew Ross, 2018

1

A troubled childhood

'I had no love from my mother at all'

NINETEEN HUNDRED AND FIFTEEN proved to be a plentiful year for the birth of well-known actors, actresses and singers. A quick glimpse through the year reveals the arrival into the world of many famous names from the past including Frank Sinatra, Edith Piaf and Orson Welles.

In Britain, while World War One raged, numerous other famous icons were also born including comedians Sir Norman Wisdom and Dick Emery and stars of the silver screen such as Michael Denison, Patricia Roc and Phyllis Calvert.

It was in Southend-on-Sea, in Essex, that Margaret Rose Mount was born on 2nd May 1915.[1] The second daughter of Alfred and Rose, and better known as Peggy Mount, she would go on to become one of the most successful actresses of her generation.

Peggy's father, Alfred John Mount, was born in Whitstable, Kent, in 1874, the son of Edward Mount and his wife Sarah Ann (née Camburn). At the age of twenty-seven Alfred was listed in the 1901 Census as being a cheesemonger's assistant living with his twenty-one-year-old wife, Alice Emma (née Covell). Within a few short years the marriage ended with the death of Alice, at the age of just twenty-five, in 1903. After six years as a widower Alfred Mount would go on to marry Rose Penney (Penny) – a purse maker/machinist of Islington, London.

A decade her husband's junior, Rose Penney was the daughter of Henry Penney (1859-1911) and his wife Annie (née Porley, 1858-1910). Peggy's maternal grandfather spent his career running entertainments on the seafront and working as a professional comedian, under the stage name of Tom Carney. Often credited as an Irish comedian, Carney's career was remembered by his granddaughter, Nancy Mount, in 1993:

> I can remember my mother saying to me when I was young that my grandfather used to take a house in Yarmouth and work on Gorleston Pier and Wellington Pier. There were photographs there of my mother and my uncle and my grandfather. They were all performers.[2]

Ironically sixty years after Tom's death his granddaughter Nancy was still performing 'marathon stints' of piano accompaniment at Gorleston Pier. She felt the family's theatrical talents were inherited, saying: 'I think this gift is a natural gift... a wonderful gift and it comes from them. I must be steeped in it because that's all I heard about as a child.'[3]

Peggy Mount herself rarely discussed her grandfather, although in some early programmes of her theatre work he was tellingly occasionally mentioned as 'the only other member of her family who was in the theatrical profession', thus excluding her mother, her uncle and her only sister all of whom also worked in theatrical entertainment.

Peggy's only sibling, three years her senior, was her sister Nancy (born Winifred Annie Mount). Like Peggy she would attend the local school, known then as Leigh Primary School, before going on to become a gifted pianist who performed in over twenty summer seasons in various towns (including Blackpool, Newquay, Bournemouth, Clapton, South End Pier and Brighton), playing the piano on stage and 'never in the pit' and always playing music by memory without sheet music.

In her old age Nancy would recall how their mother also sang and played the piano throughout her life. She also recalled Rose's last appearance as a singer – on which occasion Nancy accompanied her mother through a forty-verse song – revealing that Rose 'remembered it all' and 'stole the show … she was marvellous'.[4]

Peggy Mount's memories of her father were vague. Throughout her childhood, he suffered from chronic ill health as a result of the wasting disease locomotor ataxia and she would later recall that he was 'an invalid… a very, very, very sick man. I never really knew him as well as I'd like to because he was such a sick man.'[5] Despite this distant relationship Peggy, in the words of writer Pam Valentine, 'worshipped her father', even decades after his death.[6] For some time Alfred managed a grocery shop not far from the family home at 15 East Street, Leigh-on-Sea, but unlike his in-laws had no theatrical interests whatsoever. Of the talent inherited by his daughters, Nancy would dismissively admit: 'It didn't come from my father – he had no music in him at all.'[7]

Alfred's illness meant that his ability to work was restricted and as a result the Mount family faced financial hardship. His wife often performed professionally as a singer in order to supplement the family's income. She would gladly regale her eldest daughter with stories about the many shows she performed in and was remembered by Nancy as 'a wonderful woman'.[8]

The family's economic difficulties left their mark on Peggy. Throughout her life, and despite the financial rewards that came with her eventual success as an actress, Peggy remained 'sensible' with money. She was not in the least ostentatious and although she was later able to maintain two homes (in central London and in her native town) she was careful not to live extravagantly. Her one-time co-star, Ayshea Brough, would later remember that Peggy 'dressed very simply and drove a very ordinary car' and she remained modest and homely until the very end of her life.[9] Certain possessions were treasured; for example, a pair of black clip-on earrings was kept for some forty years and Peggy was frequently photographed wearing them. Likewise her simple taste in home décor was recalled by Harry Darton, who later inherited the 'Mr Benn' figures Peggy had collected and kept in the kitchen of her London home. Even when established as a star, Peggy's dressing room would be modestly decorated with a selection of teacups (because, in the words of actor Mark Curry, 'she *loved* a cuppa') and one or two cherished photographs, notably in character as the Nurse in Zeffirelli's production of *Romeo and Juliet* (with Dame Judi Dench) and in the title role of *Mother Courage*.[10]

After years of poor health Alfred Mount died at his home in the presence of his wife on 15th April 1930. He was fifty-six years old and his official cause of death was given as locomotor ataxia (also known as tabes dorsalis). This devastating wasting illness results in the inability to precisely control bodily movements, as a result of degeneration of the spinal column. The disease itself is caused by syphilis and may appear up to twenty years after the initial infection, eventually resulting in an extensive range of symptoms including shooting pains, emaciation, loss of muscular coordination and loss of reflexes.

The death of Alfred Mount was a crushing blow and changed the dynamics of the family forever. Peggy, then aged less than fifteen, was forced to leave school to help support the family by working as a clerk and later as a secretary for what was then Southend Corporation. It was not an easy life with one journalist going so far as to say her formative years were a 'misery'. Undoubtedly Peggy never quite recovered from her father's death which, combined with her mother's inhibited behaviour towards her, had a massive impact on her ability to form relationships throughout her life. Local resident Beryl Schofield met Peggy during the war when they were both entertaining the troops and was friends with both Mount sisters. With first-hand knowledge of the family she would admit of Peggy in 2001: 'She had a very difficult childhood, both her and her sister, but both of them survived.'[11]

The economic difficulties of the Mount family were exacerbated by the difficult relationship between Peggy and her mother. Rose Mount was to be a major influence in her daughter's life. Despite their mutual interest in entertainment Peggy would admit in her final years:

> I had nothing in common with my mother at all – I wouldn't know what it was to have an arm round me and be loved from my mother.

I never really had any [physical] contact with her. She didn't like me
particularly. I had no love from my mother at all.

Despite such lack of affection Peggy conceded: 'I don't
think it has affected me greatly. I was very fortunate in that
sense that it didn't embitter me…'[12]

According to Peggy, her father's ill health meant that she
received attention from friends and neighbours who took
sympathy on the family; indeed she would admit that she had
a 'wonderful childhood because everyone was so kind to me',[13]
but it was her sister who was clearly the apple of Rose Mount's
eye as Peggy would recall:

My older sister was always held up as an example to me. I lived
entirely in her shadow. My mother told me I was wicked and
worthless. Now, when I look back, it is clear that my mother never
loved me. She didn't even like me, and I grew up without affection
or love from her.[14]

Aside from the tragic death of her father in 1930, the most
dramatic event of Peggy's childhood involved a bizarre
accident, which resulted in severe scalding to her legs and feet.
In 1996, Peggy would recount the story, describing how her
childhood fear of the dark led her to lock the door after Nancy
had gone out to get coal for the fire. As Peggy turned she
accidentally knocked over a boiling kettle of water, which
directly hit her feet and legs. She admitted that her boots
became 'water boots' and that through rubbing her leg the dye
from her brown woollen stockings went into her skin and
poisoned her. Her recovery was slow, and so severe was the
injury her doctor wanted to amputate one of her legs. It was
only the attention of a Scottish nurse who told the doctor 'You

are too fond of taking people's limbs off' that prevented such drastic action from being taken. The wound was dutifully dressed three times a day and Peggy's leg was ultimately saved. Once recovered the physical change in Peggy was clear for all to see and she revealed: 'I went to bed with that bad leg a little fragile child and got out of bed fat. It shocked all my glands, it must have done.'[15]

Peggy's weight gain caused her intense personal unhappiness, not helped by the alleged taunts she received from her mother. Opening up about the issue at the end of her life Peggy admitted of her mother: 'She was always telling me that I was overweight and ugly. If you're told that often enough, you become ugly, and no matter what other people say you believe it.' The psychological effects of her mother's words never left Peggy. Throughout her life she remained highly conscious of both her looks and weight and, while never vain, remained conscious of her size until the very end of her life. Actress Penny Ryder worked with Peggy in the 1980s and remembers the story of Peggy's childhood accident and how she had once been 'very skinny but then became ill and gained weight'.[16] The story was also recounted by Peggy at the age of eighty-one on radio in *Desert Island Discs*; and although she claimed at that stage her weight 'did not matter', listening to her reminiscences it is clear that the issue was still paramount in her mind and deeply heartfelt.

It is perhaps not surprising, given her difficult and seemingly unhappy childhood, that Peggy would look for an escape from the realities of her young life. This was at the beginning of the Great Depression and times for the Mount family continued to be difficult. Peggy's local Wesleyan chapel provided a haven for the teenager. In amateur dramatics she was able to flee the company of her mother and older sister; and it was under the guidance and supervision of Phyllis Reader, a qualified teacher of speech and drama, that Peggy became the queen of the 'AmDrams' in Southend. Peggy always had a flair for performing and claimed that her amateur career began at the age of five. Once she had left school and was working Peggy would attend the local theatre whenever she could, buying 'late doors' tickets sold five minutes before curtain up, with 3d saved from her wages. She also occasionally ventured to London to see bigger productions.

Despite success in amateur dramatics, Peggy remained in her elder sibling's shadow. In her 1996 *Desert Island Discs* interview with Sue Lawley, Peggy described her sister as a 'brilliant pianist' and again used the same adjective to describe Nancy's rise to success within the music industry at the time. Despite her success in amateur productions it was clear that Peggy felt unable to compete in many ways with her elder sibling 'who was going to go to the top of the tree', and she admitted that in some respects this left her with a 'shocking inferiority complex... but never about my work'.[17]

Peggy's journey up the acting ladder is very similar to those of a number of her contemporaries. Financial hardship meant that it was impossible for her to train at a drama school or college. She would learn her craft 'on the job' , not least of all by ultimately spending almost fifteen years in weekly rep with a variety of companies in Chester, Wolverhampton, Liverpool, Windsor and Worthing. Playing an incredible array of roles, this was acting at its toughest and not for the faint-hearted. By her early twenties she was an established performer and in

1937 it was reported in the local press that she had entertained over sixty children at a Coronation tea party in South Fambridge along with Miss Stella Lockwood, Mrs Lockwood and Mr Hoare.[18]

As soon as she was able to, Peggy escaped the home life that had made her miserable for so long. Choosing to largely obliterate the dark days of her youth from her memory, she hardly ever spoke of her childhood, and when she did the details of her relationship with her mother and sister were rarely mentioned. Actor Mark Curry, who became friends with Peggy after working with her in the 1990s, remembers: 'Peggy confided in me that her childhood days weren't particularly happy. She became much happier as a performer and felt that her theatre colleagues were her real family.'[19] By the end of the Second World War, by which time she was gaining constant work as an actress, Peggy brought down the curtain on her mother and sister. Their relationship, in Peggy's mind at least, simply ceased to exist.

2
Treading the boards

'The wilderness years'

DURING THE LATTER HALF of the 1930s and throughout the 1940s Peggy built up her acting experience with a range of repertory companies. In doing so she toured the country, staying in numerous towns and cities and a wide variety of boarding houses and 'digs'. These were, as one fan later commented, her 'wilderness years'. Many of the actors Peggy performed alongside quickly disappeared into the depths of theatrical history; indeed, few went on to become established actors in any medium when the boom period of repertory theatre began to decline. Some were slightly luckier and went on to pursue steady careers as jobbing actors, without ever becoming big 'names' or achieving stardom. It is purely speculative to suppose that Peggy too may not have become a great name in British acting had it not been for the phenomenal success she later achieved on stage (see Chapter 3). However, it seems unlikely she would have ever given up on her career as an actress. She may well have gone on to become a familiar mainstay in theatre and perhaps television, in the vein of other distinctive actresses, such as Queenie Watts or Ann Lancaster, who became recognisable faces but could never be classified as 'stars'.

Peggy's desire to perform was in her blood and it is worth remembering that her elder sister, although never famous on the same scale as Peggy, continued to entertain and work until the very end of her long life. It is quite likely that if stardom had eluded Peggy she may well have followed in Nancy's footsteps by looking into different avenues of the profession. She may well have become a drama coach, or even pursued a career behind the curtain in stage management or production. Thankfully Peggy's years in repertory allowed her to spread her wings and complete her arduous apprenticeship in the best possible way.

On several occasions it was reported in the local press that the Mount sisters had worked together, including at the Garrison Theatre – Nancy as pianist and Peggy as compere.[20] During the 1940s Nancy was signed to Southend Cliffs Entertainment and was in demand for various entertainment events. From that point onwards she became well known, at least locally. For many years she was the resident pianist at the Sun Deck Theatre on Southend Pier and also toured the country.

In 1955, when she was forty-three years old, it was reported in local news that Nancy had married for the first time, to Edward Charles Collins. It was the last occasion on which

Nancy would be regarded as the more famous of the Mount sisters. Despite becoming Mrs Collins, for the majority of her life Nancy was known by her stage name of Nancy Mount (official records list her under various names including Nancy Winifred Collins, Winifred Collins and Nancy Mount). Her relatively late marriage did not last, although she did not appear to divorce. Like many aspects of her life she kept this period private. Her friends Philip and Sally Brazier only remember Nancy briefly mentioning her failed marriage on one occasion when she told them the union ended because 'he loved me too much'.[21] For a number of years Nancy and her husband ran their own theatrical agency covering all the main council, club and private functions in Essex, Suffolk and Norfolk. The business partnership the couple ran was dissolved in 1966.

It appears that as the 1940s progressed, and as Peggy began to gain steady employment as an actress, her relationship with her elder sister finally broke down. One local source claims that the sisters set up a music business together and its subsequent failure resulted in Peggy 'hating' her sister. This seems unlikely. By all accounts it was not in Peggy's nature to hate, although she became increasingly adept at bringing down the curtain on relationships whenever she felt offended or even slighted. Fundamentally she was a kind and giving person; always hospitable especially when it came to feeding friends and colleagues, although she increasingly disliked profuse thanks for any act of generosity. Likewise, Nancy appears to have been a compassionate and gregarious person. Her close friends Harry and Joan Maggs were aware that she had 'fallen out' with Peggy but didn't know any details surrounding the troubled relationship. They would describe Nancy as 'very private and loving'.[22] Philip and Sally Brazier were also aware that the Mount sisters had fallen out, admitting: 'Nancy would never speak about her sister. [We] never really got to the bottom of this but I understand that Peggy was a bit of a rebel.'[23]

While the difficult relationship between the sisters was certainly common knowledge to many local residents, with journalist Roger Diss writing in the local press in 1978 that Peggy 'never sees her sister', it remained a mystery to those dearest to Peggy.[24] Eira Griffiths (Darton), who for the last thirty years of Peggy's life was one of her closest friends, was a prime example of someone to whom the relationship remained veiled in ambiguity. She recalls: 'We never actually knew but there was a betrayal of some kind, or so she thought, and she could never reconcile herself to family life.' Peggy's ability to cut off people, even blood relations, was summed up by Eira in 2017:

> If people disappointed her, or did things she thought were not right, that was it. She scissored in her mind and cut them off – and this is what she did with her family. I never knew what they did that so appalled her; we never knew that side of her.[25]

The Mount sisters were certainly very different in many ways, even physically. Although neither was slim from the time they reached adulthood, it is clear that Nancy was the more attractive of the two ladies. John Holmes would recall that to him she always seemed 'heavily made up' whereas Peggy rarely wore make-up, except when on stage.[26] Both ladies were dark haired but in later years Nancy would artfully dye her hair a luxurious shade of dark chocolate brown (even in her nineties) and would also occasionally wear a wig. Peggy on the other hand never dyed her hair and after having it cut in her forties kept the same style, more or less, for the next four decades. Nancy was noted for her grand fashion sense whereas Peggy had an entirely different and less 'flashy' attitude towards clothing and fashion.

Although never as ostentatious as her elder sister in her appearance, it has to be said that Peggy enjoyed looking her best, and in particular wearing stylish jewellery. Actor Mark Curry, who became friends with Peggy in her old age, admits: 'Despite never playing what you would call "glamorous" roles, offstage she really enjoyed dressing smartly and wearing lovely dangling earrings and jewellery whenever we had to attend functions whilst on the road.'[27]

Nevertheless, generally speaking, Peggy was often at her happiest in a pinafore while entertaining friends. Physically lighter than Peggy, Nancy also had a lighter voice with a distinctive Essex accent. What is obvious, however, is that both ladies had strong personalities and a desire to enjoy the limelight and take centre stage. It is perhaps possible that their dominating personas simply clashed too much and in the end resulted in a complete breakdown of relations. Their long-standing feud surely rivalled the most famous sibling falling-out in show-business history between Olivia de Havilland and her younger sister Joan Fontaine (who famously remained at odds with each other for sixty years), yet such was the discretion of the two sisters that the feud has never been written about or particularly discussed.

General sibling rivalry and Peggy's sudden but sustained rise to stardom may also partly account for their frosty relationship. Writer Alan Bennett met Nancy in 1966 when she was hired as a pianist for his television play *On the Margin*. He would later recall: 'My only recollection of Nancy is that she slightly resented her sister's reputation,' although he also admits, 'I may be doing her an injustice though!'[28]

Peggy's early years undoubtedly impacted on her ability to form relationships throughout her life. Eira Griffiths would reveal:

Her manner protected her from feeling too much for other people… she didn't want to get involved emotionally – it was a defence mechanism, but she was very sympathetic – she just couldn't convey it somehow.[29]

Both Peggy and Nancy remained very tight-lipped about their 'feud' and it wasn't until both ladies were in their eighties that they shed some light on their relationship – although it has to be said that so little was revealed that any real assessment of the estrangement remains purely speculative.

On 6th November 1993 Nancy Mount was interviewed at her home for BBC Radio Essex by Ric Morgan. She was unable to make it into the studio due to work commitments, which took up most of her time and especially Saturday nights when she was constantly performing in concerts and cabaret in addition to tutoring a number of pupils. As well as playing a couple of songs on the piano, including 'Unforgettable' and 'Crazy for You', Nancy spoke of her theatrical/musical roots and the 'wonderful gift' she had been given, passed on through her grandfather and her mother. She spoke of the many names from the past with whom she had worked, including singer Adelaide Hall (who ironically died the following day) and ventriloquist Ray Alan, and revealed she was still occasionally working on television (notably with Mike Reid on a television documentary in her eighties).

Nancy clearly followed her sister's career; she admitted to hearing Peggy on the radio and knew that she was rehearsing for *Blithe Spirit*, and was also aware that she had been in the area at Christmas (1992/93) for pantomime. She praised her younger sibling and her 'wonderful way of going on – she's got the gift hasn't she? We're all very proud.' Linking back to their theatrical roots Nancy would say, 'I expect they're all watching from the heavens and thinking how proud they must be of her. Marvellous.'

Perhaps tellingly, when the interviewer described Peggy as 'larger than life', Nancy would reply, 'That's the word, dear – you've got it.' Those brief words were Nancy's last (known) recorded memories of her younger sister. It was Peggy who was to have the final say on their connection.

Three years later, in her 1996 *Desert Island Discs* interview with Sue Lawley, Peggy was questioned about her relationship with Nancy. She quickly brushed aside the issue, saying, 'I haven't seen her for years… we never really kept in contact.'[30] The interview amazed many of Peggy's friends and colleagues who, unlike many residents of Leigh-on-Sea, were blissfully unaware that she had a sister. Ian Talbot, a close friend during the last twenty years of Peggy's life, recalls: 'I didn't even know she had a sister until I listened to *Desert Island Discs* in 1996.'[31] At that time Nancy, then aged eighty-four, was Peggy's closest living relative and in robust good health. Yet even in the twilight of their lives the sisters would not be reconciled. The true cause of the long-standing rift would remain a secret that the sisters would take to their graves.

In the same interview Peggy would sum up her attitude towards her family by describing a plaque in the kitchen of her London home, inscribed with the words:

God gives us our relations – thank God we can choose our friends.

* * *

Nancy Mount went on to share her passion for music, both as a performer and as a teacher, throughout her extraordinarily long life. She was well-loved by many of her neighbours, a number of whom became good friends, especially in her latter years. Like many of Nancy's friends, Philip and Sally Brazier were not privy to the details as to why the Mount sisters became estranged. They remember that Nancy was keen to 'keep the past very private'.[32] Another friend was Nick Corrigan, who was taught to play the piano by Nancy after he saw her advert in the local newspaper for a 'teacher in need of pupils'. Nancy was eighty-eight years old at the time and continued to teach Nick every week until her sudden death eleven years later. Like the Braziers he would remember Nancy with deep affection, as a 'private individual' with whom he shared 'some good and fun times'. Although Nick recalled 'talking of her past and her former friends' he admits 'in all honesty we spoke very rarely of Peggy'.[33]

Nancy spent her entire life living in Southend where she was reasonably well known even in her old age. Philip and Sally Brazier were two people whose lives were particularly touched by Nancy, as they recalled to the author:

We had a very good relationship with Nancy and knew of her since moving in next door but one, thirty-two years ago. It would be fair to say that she was 'quite a character' with her eccentricities and her ways. She would dress flamboyantly when she went out to play the piano in local restaurants and as she got older this never changed. As she became older and less able to go out to the restaurants she took it upon herself to teach our four girls the piano, which was more of a social occasion, and they all held a mutual love and respect for her. She would never charge them any money for their lessons but they would always leave with some sweets or a 'KitKat'. She also had her regular students, one of whom had Down's Syndrome, and was in fact teaching him right up until the day before she died at age ninety-nine.

Nancy remained the 'show person' into her old age and every Christmas we would have a piano recital where all her students would be invited to play a piece in front of an audience which consisted of neighbours and various others she would invite. As her flat was quite small these recitals were held in our house until more people were invited and we had to borrow a church hall.

Some years ago she was interviewed by Radio Essex and recounted her stories and anecdotes of her time in show business. Over the years however these tales would get more and more exaggerated so you didn't really know what to believe in the end.

Nothing was ever ordinary with Nancy; for example her dresses 'had been flown in from Paris' (doubtful), or one of her students was 'the head of Social Services' (he wasn't, he works in the finance department).

Nancy had no time for doctors or medicine but reluctantly agreed for the GP to visit at one time to check on her health. She only agreed to let him in because he told her he wouldn't get paid otherwise. She refused his help but instead regaled him with her stories and packed him off with a KitKat.[34]

Harry and Joan Maggs were also touched by Nancy's significant influence. They would recall her as 'an incredibly kind piano teacher' who taught their son James to play the keyboard, and as a 'truly remarkable and kind lady and a special friend'. Like the Braziers they were kind enough to share their thoughts on a lady who was clearly a considerable personality in her own right:

James has Down's Syndrome and Nancy was very fond of him, spending many years during the later stages of her life to support his musicality.

Every Monday at 4pm she would give him a one-hour lesson. Nancy taught James to play the electric keyboard to a standard where he could perform as an entertainer to paying audiences, playing a repertoire of songs in musical cabaret style. Songs such as, 'Don't Bring Lulu', as well as ABBA songs, also 'Bridge Over Troubled Water' etc. Nancy taught James melody lines as well as the accompaniment, including programming percussion and drum tracks, and he was able to select and play to a very high standard because of her excellent tuition.

James was initially offered the opportunity to play one or two numbers from Nancy's set-list whilst she was performing in old people's homes. Her favourite tune was 'A Nightingale Sang in Berkeley Square' which she played beautifully.

Nancy was an inspiration and a mentor to James and she proved to be a vital link between his abilities and the opportunity for others to hear and share in both of their musical gifts. Nancy was very strict and very kind – a combination that supported him to perform so well that he was booked for his own one-hour shows, to finally taking on her portfolio of venues, as a performer in his own right.

Nancy supported James with a strong work ethic and 'the show must go on' approach. Whatever was happening in her life she kept a positive attitude and was always well presented in full make-up, dark hair, blue/green eye make-up, courting red lipstick. Looking good was important to Nancy! This influenced James to also wear tuxedos and have costume changes when performing on stage.

James was very caring of Nancy and a wonderful and reciprocal friendship evolved because of her unbelievable kindness and patience. She would comment, 'You can't rush James,' yet she managed over the many years of lessons to propel him forward with confidence and musicality, even booking church halls to put on her own shows, featuring her music students, both young and old.

Nancy lived alone in a flat, in the top half of a house in Pall Mall, Leigh-on-Sea, Essex. She was supported by friendly neighbours and was able to continue living independently, aided by a helper called Sharon, who had grown up knowing Nancy. The flats were separated by their own front doors but the house originally belonged, we believe, to Nancy who much later had a chair-lift fitted to ascend to the upper floor.

Her upstairs small room was the 'music room' housing the electric keyboards, but she had ornaments of pianos in every room including a big upright piano in her living room. On the wall opposite the keyboards was a picture of a gentleman who she said was a performer who had inspired her; and overlooking everything was an enormous gilt-framed picture of her mother. Family was important to Nancy, and she was respectful of others' beliefs and encouraged kindness. James was brought up as a Jehovah's Witness, and Nancy told him she was a Christadelphian which contributed to her continual positive attitude; in times of challenges, she told him to cover himself with a 'blanket of love' and that he would be looked after.

Nancy taught James with a full one hour's lesson on the night before she died, watching and waving to him at the window in her usual fashion as he walked down the garden path with his mother before stepping into his father's red Toyota car parked outside and waving back up to her.

The lady living in the downstairs flat said Nancy was playing the keyboards until 11.30pm the night before she died, which was highly unusual – almost like she knew it was her last chance to play. James tells us that during his lesson that day he played his favourite song, 'Amarillo'; then Nancy suggested that he played 'The Day You Loved Me' by Katherine Jenkins, followed by 'Time to Say Goodbye'.[35]

Nancy Mount died suddenly but peacefully in her sleep on 18th May 2011. In true show-business style she had always remained coy about her age and those closest to her were 'stunned' to discover that she was ninety-nine years old. In her Last Will and Testament she would remember her friends and pupils, with many inheriting token sums of money and musical instruments.

Nancy's death, almost a decade after that of her younger sister, went quietly unnoticed by the press. A small obituary would announce that her funeral service was to be held at Southend Crematorium, South Chapel, on Wednesday 22nd June, over a month after her death, but there was no mention of her famous sister or indeed of her long career in local entertainment.[36] Despite her belief that Nancy would become a star in the entertainment industry it was ultimately Peggy who would achieve national and international fame.

* * *

By the latter stages of the Second World War Peggy was busy performing at concert parties and working with ENSA, sometimes giving up to three or four performances a day for the troops. When peace finally came to Britain in 1945 Peggy's career really began to develop, and shortly after the end of the war she was approached by Jan Fogarty, who ran the Harry Hanson company at the Palace Theatre, Westcliff-on-Sea.

Their encounter happened as Peggy was sitting in a café awaiting an evening performance at the theatre and, almost like a scene from a 1940s movie, this meeting proved to be a turning point in her life and career. Fogarty asked if Peggy would work professionally at Hanson's theatre in Keighley in Yorkshire, to which she gladly said yes. Slightly bemused by the request, Peggy asked why she had been singled out, to which Fogarty replied: 'Amateurs are a pain in the arse, always wanting to borrow things and never coming to our plays. I've been hearing all about you, but you've never once pestered us. That's why.' Peggy would later admit that it was a 'strange' way to start a professional career in the theatre, but taking Jan Fogarty up on the offer was something she would never regret.[37]

South African-born Harry Hanson was regarded as the last of the 'circuit' managers in weekly repertory theatres. By the time of his death at the age of seventy-seven in 1972, weekly reps were almost extinct; but for decades he helped to provide employment for hundreds of actors, stage managers and theatre staff, in addition to entertaining regional audiences up and down the country. After forming the 'Harry Hanson Court Players' at Hastings in 1932, Hanson went on to form further companies at Leeds, Sheffield, Peterborough, Penge, Nottingham, Richmond, Stockton, Chester, Bradford and Swansea. Although well known for his short temper, Hanson was admired by Peggy and years later she would describe him to author Kate Dunn:

> He was a little, short, fat man and he had three wigs. One wig was blonde and if he was wearing that you kept out of his way because he was in a bad mood; a grey wig and he was all right; he had another one and if he wore that you knew that everybody was happy and nobody would get sacked.[38]

Peggy's first foray into repertory theatre began with her arriving in Keighley in pouring rain late on a Sunday night in 1945. Brought up as a Methodist and forced to sign the pledge, she would later reminisce about being taken to a local pub, where she drank shandy for the first time ever, and then playing in the 'beautiful little theatre there – twice weekly, twice nightly rep – for four pounds a week with two pound ten going on digs, bed and breakfast'.[39]

For the next decade Peggy was constantly busy working in repertory theatre up and down the country. It was the hardest way to learn her craft but set her in good stead for the lifelong career she would ultimately enjoy. Among the countless actors with whom she performed at this time, only a handful went on to sustain acting careers for many more years, perhaps most notably David Stoll (who enjoyed a long stage career, being considered 'the best farceur in the country' by Miriam Karlin) and William Moore, the future husband of actress Mollie Sugden, who remained busy on stage and television and memorably co-starred with his wife in the 1980s sitcom *My Husband and I.*

During her years in rep Peggy frequently made the news, albeit in a minor way. There are literally dozens of reviews that mention her name in various minor roles in plays in which she toured the provinces during the late 1940s. Generally they are positive but rarely outstanding. A small selection follows:

In the satirical comedy *The Best People* (1945) she had a 'minor role' as Miss Tate but gave a 'clever performance' at the Royalty Theatre, Gloucester (*The Chronicle*, 10th November 1945).

In *Indian Summer* she 'maintains the high standard of the acting' (*The Cheshire Observer*, 17th November 1945).

In 1946 at the Theatre Royal, Leeds, she was 'very effective' as the maid in *George and Margaret* (*The Yorkshire Post,* 3rd September 1946).

Three years later in August 1949 her 'fussy, tearful' Aunt Hatty in *The House of Women* made enough of an impression for one critic to comment that she would be 'an asset to the company' (*The Courier and Advertiser*, 9th August 1949).

In October 1949 'the acting was worthy of the play, with the honours going to Miss Peggy Mount as Lady Kitty, a woman whose memories of "one crowded hour" are worth all the heartache and tears. Miss Mount's performance was impeccable' (*The Montrose Review,* 21st October 1949).

Much was made of Peggy's work during the Second World War. It was reported in 1949 that she had 'gained a lot of experience as a member of concert parties during the war'. On one occasion she was involved in a tour of Essex, organised at short notice so that the troops could be entertained on a certain night. It was only afterwards that the artistes realised that they had been helping to brighten up the evening before D-Day (*The Evening Telegraph,* 30th September 1949).

At this relatively early stage in her career Peggy admitted to the press that she was particularly fond of character parts. Among her favourite roles were Madame Arcati in *Blithe Spirit* (a role, ironically, that she would play on numerous occasions in later years), Judith in *Hay Fever* and Catherine in *Arms and the Man* (*The Evening Telegraph,* 30th September 1949)

By August 1950 she had joined the Liverpool Playhouse Company and made an immediate impression in *The Brothers Castiglioni* at the Liverpool Playhouse with one critic writing: 'Newcomers who impress favourably are Peggy Mount; as a buxom Latin scold' (*The Stage,* 24th August 1950).

A small break from the seemingly endless cycle of rep came in the winter of 1951 when Peggy was cast to appear as the Witch in Val Parnell's pantomime production of *Humpty Dumpty* at the London Palladium. The cast included Terry-Thomas (as King Felicia) and the future *Crossroads* star Noele Gordon (as Captain Florizel). It was by far one of Peggy's most notable appearances to date. Although it would be some years before Peggy would become a star in London's West End, this appearance marked a turning point in her career and was her first significant appearance in a major London theatre.

Peggy's involvement in *Humpy Dumpy* was fondly remembered by Jean Bayliss (playing Princess Miranda), who went on to become the first British actress to play Maria Von Trapp in *The Sound of Music* on stage. In 2017, her youthfulness belying her eighty-six years, Jean would recall Peggy's 'rasping laugh' to the author and that her co-star would 'sit on the floor of Norman's [Evans] dressing room – legs apart in her witch's costume – eating lovely pies and food that Norman's wife used to stuff us with'. Jean would recall the long run, with daily matinees, as 'quite exhausting' but that the cast 'always met to eat in Norman's room'.[40]

* * *

Once established as a star actress in her forties, Peggy would frequently discuss the pros and cons of work in repertory theatre. She preferred three-week runs, which were rare, rather than weekly rep, because they gave her the opportunity to fine tune a performance. 'There is so much hit and miss,' she once said, 'but with all that, it is invaluable experience which no actor or actress should miss. You learn so many things the hard way – which is best. You learn to understand so many kinds of audience, develop your memory in a way impossible elsewhere and learn to carry on under all sorts of difficult circumstances.'[41]

The whole experience of touring the country, living in digs and learning lines at breakneck speed was invaluable to Peggy.

From an early age she would learn that the dynamics of the company impacted greatly upon the play – and its success. Likewise, in addition to inevitable clashes of personality, Peggy also had to cope with frequent last-minute changes in scripts, changes in props and changes in scenery. She also worked as ASM (Assistant Stage Manager) during her years in rep and later admitted: 'Assistant stage manager sounds wonderful but you were just a dogsbody. I even scrubbed the stage.'[42] It was far from a glamorous life, but was the greatest learning curve of her career and she revelled in it.

Moving from town to town and living in digs had occasional benefits. She was often embraced by local residents and business owners and would recall to author Kate Dunn how a local butcher in Chester 'loved her' and would bring her steak, for free, during the long years of meat rationing.[43] Regional landladies meanwhile provided a huge source of inspiration for the many characters she would play in the years to come. Resourcefulness was an essential element of the world of rep and she later admitted: 'If you had an evening dress in a play one week, next week you'd turn it inside out and use it as a dressing gown.'[44]

It was in repertory, at a relatively early age, that Peggy was given the harsh truth about her looks and weight. Throughout her life she remained conscious of her size, her toothy grin, her large chin and homely looks. Despite being astute enough to know that her career and wealth were based partly on her physical appearance, she often yearned to be slimmer and more attractive. She was after all only human. In 1955, having achieved stardom in the theatre, she would reveal:

From one [first class] director I learned a particularly vital thing –
how to straighten out my ideas about being a leading lady. When I
was about 30, a director warned me that I would never be a leading
lady in the ordinary sense, adding that I had better put all such ideas
out of my head and concentrate on being a character woman. How
right he was! Ever since then I have avoided as much as possible
playing any part unsuited to my face and figure.[45]

Years later Peggy would admit it was in fact company
manager and director Jeffrey Wood who had spoken to her
about her physical appearance when he saw her in Leeds eating
an apple because she 'wanted to get thin and play the
glamorous parts'. She was advised by Wood that she had 'a
character face, a character body, a character walk' and that she
would never be 'anything but a character woman – so eat!'

This piece of advice, which at the time reduced Peggy to
tears, never left her. For years she had struggled with her
weight and believed that if she slimmed down enough and 'was
a good enough actress' she could play glamorous roles.[46] Over
the decades there were several occasions during which she
would make a conscious effort to shed extra pounds – with
limited success. A love of food and cooking meant that Peggy
would never be a svelte lady, regardless of the thyroid problem
she claimed to suffer from throughout her life. As the years
progressed both Peggy (and to a degree those closest to her)
became slightly less conscious of her size although it would
always be something which troubled her.

By the time she became a star in her forties Peggy's most
distinctive feature was her voice. According to the actress
herself, it was her long and intense run in *Sailor, Beware!*
which caused a permanent change to her voice; and perhaps,
too, her long years in repertory theatre inevitably impacted

upon her vocal cords. She claimed to have started *Sailor, Beware!* with 'a beautiful contralto velvety voice' but admitted: 'Three years in the play in the West End... with fifteen hundred people all laughing their heads off – I had to go over the top of them and of course I finished up with a very rough voice.' Peggy conceded that her voice simply 'got rougher and rougher' with the passage of time.[47]

However, as early as 1950 her ability to shout had already become something of a trademark. Her role in the first-ever English stage production of *The Beaver Coat* at the Liverpool Playhouse brought her good reviews as 'an energetic, rip-roaring Juno, dominating her husband, her family and most of the village community with both voice and brains', although it was also noted that 'John Barry matches Miss Mount when it comes to shouting.'[48]

Many of Peggy's colleagues were aware of her unique vocal talent and would remember it in different ways. For Sir Ian McKellen it led to a particularly memorable conversation with Peggy:

> She told me that during the Blitz she managed to get a lift home after public transport had stopped. She chatted all the way from London to Southend but, because of the blackout, never saw her obliging driver whose parting words, as he dropped her safely at her front door, were, 'It's been a pleasure to listen to your beautiful voice through the whole journey.' Peggy's voice was of course distinctive but scarcely beautiful. I still don't know whether that was the point of the story.[49]

Critics quickly latched on to Peggy's unique vocal gift, and her imposing physical stature, with *The Times* regarding her as 'more intimidating than a fixed bayonet... with a voice to match'[50] whilst *The Guardian* would write that her voice 'could have made a regimental sergeant major tremble' and her figure 'wordlessly and hilariously forbade the taking of liberties'.[51]

* * *

It seems likely that Peggy's one real chance at romance occurred during her years in repertory. Ultimately she never married and did not have children. Throughout her life she remained fairly tight-lipped about potential suitors. In 1996 she hinted at past dalliances saying, 'I've never married but I worked with a lot of very eligible men and I've had my chances.' She also conceded that her formative years may have impacted on her decision to remain single, saying, 'I do think my mother's love-less[ness] probably did have a lot to do with it,' while admitting both publicly and privately that she would have struggled to maintain a career as a star actress if she had married.[52]

Ayshea Brough worked with Peggy in 1981 and would recall: 'I'm not sure whether she fell for someone when she was very young… I had the feeling that she did and never got over it and being a very plain woman, if we're honest, that was not easy. Although there is a lid for every pot she remained on her own.'[53]

Actress Damaris Hayman agrees that it seems likely that Peggy would have experienced some degree of male attention during her days trawling the country on stage, admitting: 'Rep is usually a sort of forcing house of flings – you are thrown together and dependent on each other,' although she boldly admits that Peggy was 'almost totally unattractive – physically and otherwise'.[54] Peggy herself would say in 1996 that, during her early days in the theatre, colleagues in a sense became her family and she found a 'wonderful fellowship in weekly rep – you *had* to have it'.[55]

Peggy's physical and vocal strength and fondness for gay male friends (of whom she had many in later years) inevitably led to some speculation regarding her own sexuality, although those who knew her well have dismissed suggestions that she may have been a lesbian; Damaris Hayman for one admits, 'I never got any suggestion that she was a lesbian.'[56] John Standing, too, when questioned about Peggy's sexuality, agrees that she 'probably wasn't a lesbian'.[57] While admitting that generally speaking Peggy 'liked having male friends' writer Pam Valentine was also well aware of Peggy's large entourage of homosexual friends, saying: 'She had a lot of gay friends and they became sort of like her family. She was always searching for a family I think – someone to love and be generous to. She was always turning up with little presents. I think she was very lonely.'[58] Others were also struck at the number of Peggy's homosexual friends, including Pat Coombs's niece, Penny Hey, who recalls:

> I met Peggy a few times, one of which was some sort of award type thingy (held in a hotel in Park Lane, I am guessing late 80s/early 90s). Pat and I were on the same table as Peggy. Peggy had a couple of male friends with her; both had been married, had children and then had 'come out'. I just remember this as being fascinating and I had the impression she had a number of gay male friends.[59]

Professionally speaking Peggy also tended to get on better with men than women. Jeffrey Holland, who worked with Peggy in the early 1970s, would recall: 'She didn't like pretty young things around; she didn't like the competition. We were all aware of that… but there was no unpleasantness.'[60]

Like Pam Valentine, actor and writer Ian Masters was also struck by both Peggy's homeliness and her personal isolation. Having toured together in *The Mating Game* in the early 1980s, including visiting Scarborough and Richmond, Ian would recall:

> She was lovely and warm in lots and lots of ways. She would make us lovely steak and kidney puddings and say, 'Come round to the digs.' Bless her. I got really fond of her; I thought she was, in some way, a sad lady because she was quite lonely I think.[61]

After a lifetime of creating emotional barriers, Peggy's characteristics did not change with age. Claudia Mayer would work with Peggy in 1987 and remembered her colleague as both 'formidable' and 'kindly' but was also aware that Peggy was a 'solitary character... she didn't allow herself to be liked'.[62]

Despite never marrying, Peggy did have a good circle of close friends. She remained increasingly careful about her private life and perhaps no one ever really got close enough to her to fully appreciate her complex character. Peggy was well aware of 'the isolation of being a star' and as a result chose her friends very cautiously. They became, in many ways, like a substitute family to her. As Eira Griffiths recalls, 'She needed to be with people who had also achieved so she didn't think they wanted something from her.'[63] Mark Curry agrees that Peggy was very selective about allowing people access to her private life: 'Peggy was fiercely loyal and protective of her friends and wary of new people during the time I knew her. We became very close but it was a gradual thing.'[64]

In time Peggy became very good friends with Norman Newell and later with Michael Evans and with Eira (Griffiths) and Harry Darton. A Golden Globe award-winning recording manager, Norman Newell was four years younger than Peggy. The pair ultimately became 'very friendly' and were often seen at celebrity events, particularly during the 1960s and 1970s. Newell's career was an enviable one. His list of 'charges' over the years included such iconic names as Dame Julie Andrews, Eartha Kitt, Dame Shirley Bassey, Sir Ken Dodd and Johnny Mathis. The pair occasionally worked together (notably in 1965 when Peggy was one of the first artists to be signed to feature on Newell's LP of *Alice in Wonderland*, released to celebrate the centenary of the publication of Lewis Carroll's famous novel) and remained friends until the end of Peggy's life.[65]

It was only really after her death that the press reported news of Peggy's 'unofficially adopted' son: Welsh-born former singer, Michael Evans. Born in 1953, Michael Evans seemingly first met Peggy when he was just fifteen years old during an audition for a television programme. Three years later, when his own mother died, he is said to have become a key part of Peggy's life. The father of twin sons, Michael suffered life-changing injuries following a fall (which resulted in him being paralysed from the neck down) and it was Peggy who helped him cope with his change in circumstances. He later said of her, 'Through all the good and bad times in my life, she's been there… My mum!' Typically, Peggy kept their relationship out of the public eye but in 1998 was quoted as saying: 'I do have a family – my adopted son Michael, his wife and two lovely children. I didn't adopt him legally but he's as much of a son as if I'd given birth. I love him dearly.'[66]

Following Peggy's death Michael (along with his sons and his wife Heather) was a beneficiary in Peggy's Last Will and

Testament. Sadly (despite repeated attempts) I have been unable to make contact with Mr Evans and as a result his relationship with Peggy has deliberately featured as a mere footnote in her biography.

Despite being friends with Peggy for decades, actress Eira Griffiths (known professionally as Eira Griffiths or sometimes as Eira Griffiths-Darton) admits she cannot remember exactly when and where she first met the lady who became a huge part of her life from the 1960s until Peggy's death. Over a decade younger than Peggy, Eira became a key member of Peggy's exclusive inner circle along with her husband, journalist Harry Darton. As the years progressed the Dartons became an essential part of Peggy's day-to-day life.

After first working with Peggy in a production of *Blithe Spirit* (and the pair would often appear in various tours of the play together) Eira admits that performing with Peggy was a 'revelation'. Although she adored Peggy, Eira was not blind to her faults and concedes that her friend was not always 'an easy person'. Despite this, their relationship, both on stage and off, was extremely harmonious and Eira confirms: 'I was no challenge to her – professionally – and that was quite good. I was never a star, I was a supporting actress and she much respected whatever I brought to a production.'[67]

Trust, of course, was the basis of their relationship and Eira would also remember that 'Norman Newell and Michael Evans were people she trusted. They treated her as a human being but also recognised her foibles.'[68] It says much for the friendship between Peggy and Eira that many of their former colleagues still remember the bond between the two ladies to this day. Eira would often understudy Peggy and have small parts in many of her plays. As Jeffrey Holland would recall, 'Peggy wouldn't go anywhere without Eira – she was always there for her.'[69]

Generally speaking Peggy did not become close friends with many of her colleagues. There were, however, a couple of notable exceptions. One of the key players to emerge from Peggy's long years in repertory was the actress Cissie Ashley, with whom Peggy worked at the beginning of her career. Cissie retired from acting in 1955 at the age of seventy, her final work having been with the Harry Hanson repertory company at Bradford. Even when she became established as a star, Peggy would remember Miss Ashley as one of the finest actors she had ever known, saying, 'She taught me so much as I watched her night after night. I owe a great deal to her.'[70] The costume designer Cecelia Doidge Ripper (who married the character actor Michael Ripper in 1995) was another 'great' friend and as a result often worked on Peggy's television shows, particularly in the 1970s; and in later years Peggy was also great chums and companions with actress Pat Coombs. On the whole, however, her inner circle was certainly not based entirely upon theatrical types. She would maintain contact with several friends in her home town into old age, and it was only when she had outlived most of her friends in Leigh-on-Sea that she decided to sell her home there.

In her sixties Peggy admitted she was happy being 'a solitary soul'[71] and again reiterated her sentiments in her eighties, saying, 'I'm quite happy by myself,' but also felt she was never lonely, once saying: 'If I get lonely... I know I have hundreds of friends so can always pick up the phone.'[72] On the subject of Peggy never marrying, her friend, actor Mark Curry, wrote:

'She never really opened up about her romances but I actually think that show business was always her first love.'[73]

3
Sailor, Beware!

'She gave me everything I ever wanted in the world'

REPERTORY THEATRE CONTINUED to be Peggy's main source of work and income as she approached her forties. By 1953, however, she had made her television debut; and the following year she played guest-house owner Mrs Larkin in John Gilling's feature film *The Embezzler*, starring Charles Victor and Zena Marshall. This was a major event in Peggy's career, catapulting her into the public domain on the big screen.

Based upon the story of a respectable bank cashier who embezzles money from the bank where he works and flees to a seaside guest-house, the film itself was well received and Peggy made an instant impression. With her long dark hair deliberately featuring grey streaks and tied neatly into a bun she was perfectly cast as the well-spoken, slightly officious landlady with a standard repertoire for each of her paying guests. Despite *The Embezzler* being Peggy's film debut it was a decent supporting role with good billing. Based upon this appearance alone it is quite likely that she could have gone on to become a busy screen actress playing similar character roles in British films throughout the boom period of the 1950s. Fate, however, led her career in a different direction.

While correspondence at the time showed that Peggy was constantly seeking work in every medium, the stage offered an array of roles and respectable notices. In 1953 her role in *Thirteen For Dinner* at the Grand Theatre, Wolverhampton, was regarded as 'versatile' and she gave a 'striking perform- ance' as a 'smouldering, avengeful Latin woman'.[74]

In the same year it was Melville Gillam of the Connaught Theatre in Worthing, Sussex who asked Peggy to read the part of Mrs Emma Hornett in *Sailor, Beware!* Very quickly Peggy realised that the role was made for her. She contacted her agent and insisted she be allowed to play the role, confidently stating: 'Nobody can do it better than me.' Peggy stayed up for three nights learning the script but her hard work paid off. From the outset the play received favourable reviews, being initially described as an 'exceptionally lively comedy, swiftly directed by Andre Van Gyseghem, and well played all round'.[75]

Written by Philip King (whose best known play was the farce *See How They Run*) and Falkland Cary (a former doctor), the play was originally tried out at the Connaught with Peggy cast as the dragon-like mother-in-law – an archetypal wife and mother who ruled her roost with ferocity and a sharp tongue. Cyril Smith was called upon to play her mild-mannered husband and additional cast members in the original run included Richard Coleman (as the bridegroom), Sheila Shand Gibbs (as Peggy's daughter), Ann Wilton (her sister-in-law), James Copeland (the best man), Anthony Marlowe (the vicar), Jean Burdess (the bridesmaid) and Myrette Morvern (as the neighbour). The plot of the slightly romantic comedy centred upon Peggy's domineering character intimidating her future son-in-law, resulting in him getting 'cold feet' on his wedding day.

Later in 1954 Peggy took on another lead role at the Connaught Theatre playing the Cockney landlady in *Beside the Seaside*, written by actor and playwright Leslie Sands. Once again working alongside Richard Coleman, Peggy was teamed with a strong cast which included Jill Dixon, John Merivale, Hazel Bainbridge and Vanda Godsell. She then went on to feature with many of the same cast members in *Because I Am Black*, a forward-thinking play about racial prejudice written by Earle Couttie (a repertory player) in which she played a guest-house proprietor 'with pleasant human touches'.[76] Thankfully the success of Peggy's portrayal in *Sailor, Beware!* was not forgotten and the popularity of the play resulted in plans to transfer the production to the West End under Jack Waller.

There are several different versions of exactly how Peggy came to be cast in the lead role of the play at the Strand Theatre in London's West End. One source states that Peggy was advised not to accept any other work in the event she may be cast to appear as Emma Hornett (and during this time, despite dwindling savings, she apparently turned down the offer of a film role with a guaranteed salary of £100 a week). It is generally accepted that Peggy was called in at the last minute to take over the role from an unnamed leading actress and in this capacity was grateful for the understanding of Andre Van Gyseghem. She later admitted:

> I was very fortunate in having someone who was so understanding. We only had five days in which to rehearse when I took over the part, and Mr Van Gyseghem let me go my own way, never trying to impose his own ideas. He helped me rather than conducting the play as a whole, as if it were a piece of music. During the second week of the run he began to offer me ideas, which, as I then knew my part, I was able to assimilate fairly easily.[77]

Peggy made her West End stage debut in *Sailor, Beware!* at the Strand Theatre on 16th February 1955. She was an instant hit with both audiences and critics alike. Within days of the play opening, Peggy's performance was hailed as 'simply terrific'. The dominant character of Emma Hornett was described as 'overdriven and flustered by circumstance, and at her best has the temper of a wounded tiger. Everyone gets the sharp edge of her tongue, though the menfolk suffer most. "You can't reason with men," says Emma firmly, "you have to train them."' High praise was also given to Peggy's co-stars, especially Richard Coleman who was described as 'most likeable as the harassed bridegroom'.[78]

Immediately reviews – both locally and nationally – were fulsome in their praise. *The Yorkshire Post and Leeds Mercury* described Emma Hornett as a 'bulldozer' of a woman 'beautifully played by Peggy Mount'[79] while *The Birmingham Post* wrote: 'Miss Mount's advance from provincial "Rep" to the London stage has been accomplished at a single triumphant leap. Her portrayal of this awesome termagent [sic] is a triumphant leap that ought to put up her name in lights without delay.'[80]

When Peggy's name did indeed go up in lights it was a thrilling memory that never left her for the next forty years. Sir Ian McKellen, who later worked with Peggy at Ipswich, would recall her overnight success:

> Before she hit stardom in *Sailor, Beware!* in the West End, Peggy's career had centred on regional repertory companies for whom she had done the out-of-town version of *Sailor, Beware!* When the London star withdrew during rehearsals, Peggy was drafted in. She was an immediate hit with the critics. She told me that after the first night, when she got off the bus to walk up to the Strand Theatre, her name had been put up in lights overnight. She stood admiring the sight, not face on, but more modestly in the reflection of a shoe shop in the Strand through which she could see her name reflected, although, of course, backwards.[81]

It is almost impossible to emphasise just how big an impact the production had on Peggy's career. Not only did she never forget the play but it was also very well remembered by the vast majority of her colleagues. In later years, for those too young to have seen the play, Peggy would frequently recount its success and the impact it had on her, often to the amusement of friends and colleagues.

Ian Talbot remembers the play's massive effect and how almost thirty years later it still remained a talking point in Peggy's life:

> Whenever she met someone she wasn't backwards in telling them that she made her name in *Sailor, Beware!* and that one day she was an unknown and the next she was a star with her name up in lights. She told the entire company this! In fact she told us every other second... We all laughed but she could take the mickey out of herself.[82]

Mark Curry was also familiar with Peggy's oft-told story:

Sailor, Beware! was her first London appearance and on the day after opening night her name was suddenly put above the title due to her rave reviews. She described turning the corner in the city, seeing her name above the title in lights and jumping into a doorway in total shock.[83]

Meanwhile reviews continued to flow in with Anthony Cookman of *The Tatler and Bystander* writing: 'Miss Mount sweeps through the performance, dominating it like an angry hurricane.'[84] While Peggy's performance was praised, the character of such a 'monumental matriarch' as Emma Hornett inevitably received mixed reactions from critics. Cookman summed up this most archetypal of mothers-in-law:

Emma Hornett is a born boss, convinced that her world is peopled by incompetents deserving to be crushed without mercy. There is only one way to do a thing. That is her way. Nobody has time to jump to her way of doing it before she has given him or her the rough edge of her tongue for being about to do it in some other way. And she has the trick of making every word tell. She is the policewoman in the home, for ever moving someone on with threats that she is well able to make good.[85]

So powerful was the image that it led to Peggy being cast in similarly strong roles for the rest of her career. As a result, to the public at large, she almost became this character: a strong, loud, short-tempered, impatient battleaxe who did not suffer fools under any circumstances.

It has to be said that this stereotype and the real-life character of Peggy Mount were not entirely dissimilar. She famously once said, 'I'm not a bit like my screen image... I don't bully. I don't shout. And, if I do have a row with somebody, it makes me ill for at least a week.'[86] In truth though Peggy never needed to 'shout'. She once admitted: 'Despite what they say, I never shout. I have a strong voice. I don't need to shout.'[87] Even without her 'strong' voice Peggy was still able to convey her mood. One look from her steely blue gaze could speak volumes. Indeed it became something of a trademark. Likewise, once established as a star actress, she did not need to 'bully'. Her word became law in many productions and she became increasingly well known within the business, quite rightly, for not tolerating unprofessionalism amongst the other actors with whom she was cast.

Mark Curry is one of many of Peggy's colleagues who would remember her no-nonsense attitude:

> Peggy could be intimidating at times. She had a slightly short fuse and didn't tolerate fools gladly. The only time she got slightly annoyed with me was when I backed our hire car into a tree whilst we were on tour together, shouting, 'How can you not see a TREE for God's sake?!!!' An overly gushing fan once got short shrift from her after a matinee at a stage door I remember. The fan enthused that they had been at school together, saying, 'Don't you remember, Peggy?' Peggy shouted, 'No! That's a long time ago. I hated school and now I'm going for my tea; come on, Mark!'[88]

While a 'real character' in her own right, Peggy also enjoyed immersing herself in the world of make-believe. Her friend Eira Griffiths would recount Peggy's attitude towards the nature of her profession, saying: 'She was very adamant in the way she portrayed things and expected that kind of concentration from others. There could be no fooling around; it was a reality for her. What she did was real.'[89]

Although never confrontational, Peggy's character, as with most, certainly had a darker side, which notably emerged in later years during her time spent working on the television sitcom *You're Only Young Twice* (see Chapter 6). Again, however, there would be no raised voices or 'scenes' from Peggy. That was not her way. She was certainly not Emma Hornett in this respect. As with her private life (so clearly seen in her relationship with her mother and sister), in her professional life Peggy would simply bring the curtain down on anyone who upset her or offended her in the slightest way. Any upset caused by personal or professional grievances was never discussed by Peggy. Her private thoughts remained entirely that – private. Even those closest to her were unable to break through the barrier she increasingly built up around her over the years.

Clearly Peggy's rise to stardom in *Sailor, Beware!* was meteoric and took everyone by surprise, not least the actress herself. Many questioned her ability to carry the play for any length of time in the West End. Happily she would prove her critics wrong and 'kept at it', admitting the audience's response to the comedy of the play helped see her through 'that long hot summer'.[90]

Peggy's long years of training had paid off. Work in provincial rep had provided her with a steady income for many years but also built up the kind of invaluable experience she needed to ultimately become a star in the theatre. In turn she never forgot her roots in repertory theatre and remained highly supportive of it, even after she had become well established as a star actress. In 1966, for example, she would go so far as to postpone production on the film *Finders Keepers* in order to be present at the Wolverhampton Repertory Company's thirtieth anniversary gala occasion.

She would later admit:

You simply must know all about your job if you are to gain confidence as well as develop your talent. Repertory teaches you not only how to play many different parts each season, but also about stage management, lighting, décor, direction and other vital elements of a production. This happens in the course of normal work, and it would not be possible, I think, to acquire so much diverse knowledge, outside of repertory theatre, at least not in the same space of time. Accidents, for instance, are one thing in repertory, quite another in a West End theatre and without my repertory experience I would not have been able to cope at the Strand.[91]

It was certainly Peggy's ability to sustain her performance week after week, month after month, which ultimately gained her star status – both within the profession and to the public at large. Actor Jeffrey Holland remembers the impact the play had on Peggy: 'She had to sign a contract but had no idea of what she was letting herself in for… She was "stuck" with the production until it finished. She had no idea it would be such a success, but was grateful for it and it did put her on the map and got her lots of other work, of course.'[92]

By March 1955 Peggy's fame had resulted in her being invited to the annual dinner of the Gallery First Nighters' Club. Amongst the guests were famous faces of the day including Margaret Leighton, Beatrice Lillie and Herbert Lom. In the same year she was asked to open Leatherhead Repertory Company's fourth annual garden party. Never one to forget her roots, Peggy also used her fame to speak out on the plight of repertory theatres and at the end of 1955, as a guest speaker at the Colchester Repertory Club, urged West End managers to form a central fund to help repertory companies. She was now mixing in the highest of acting circles.

By February 1957 *Sailor, Beware!* had celebrated its two-year run. Critics praised its longevity and its star:

Sailor, Beware!, one of the most phenomenal successes of recent years, celebrated its second anniversary at the Strand last Saturday. Few would have prophesised such a robust life for this homely farcical comedy of a mother-in-law phobia when it was first tried out at the Connaught, Worthing... All the same, this originally unstarred production has unwittingly made its own star. Peggy Mount, as the formidable Emma Hornett, with the outsize bellow, so dominates the play, as well as her hen-pecked Cyril Smith, that, from the obscurity of provincial repertory, she has become almost a national figure as, par excellence, the mother-in-law to end all mothers-in-law.

Such was the success of the play that the BBC made the rare move to broadcast it live to television viewers. The popularity of the production with the viewing public resulted in the unprecedented decision to broadcast it live for a second time, in the spring of 1957. Peggy had now emerged from being an 'obscure' repertory actress to a star of both stage and television.

In September 1957 Peggy had been ordered by doctors to take a break from the show and it was reported that she would be spending time at the coast followed by a spell in Switzerland in order to recuperate and regain her strength. The break in the gruelling schedule was a short one: she was back at the Strand by 14th September, after less than two weeks away. It was only the second time during the play's long run that Peggy was forced to withdraw. The first was the result, not surprisingly, of a sore throat and on both occasions she was temporarily replaced by Margery Fleeson. It said much for Peggy's professionalism and physical and mental strength that she was able to endure an intense and very long-lived starring performance in a West End play. *Sailor, Beware!* would set the tone for Peggy's future performances and indeed her indomitability as an actress during the rest of her career.[93]

Sailor, Beware! ran for 1,231 performances at the Strand Theatre and finally closed on 22nd February 1958. For the next forty years Peggy would look back with gratitude on the role that had made her a star, and also on her training in repertory theatre which had so well prepared her for the challenges of three years in the West End. Peggy's lead role in the play secured her position as a 'star' actress and also cemented her position in the public mind as a 'battleaxe'. Both titles would remain throughout her career.

When Peggy's appearance in *Sailor, Beware!* finally ended the success of the play was not just a critical one. It was reported that the combination of Peggy's talents and taking the play to the West End earned the authors, Philip King and Falkland Cary, a staggering '£65,000 [approximately equivalent to £1.4 million in 2018] and the expectation of a further £10,000 in repertory royalties' with 99 repertory companies having already booked it.[94] When Peggy left the role, to be replaced by the larger-than-life Welsh entertainer Tessie O'Shea, the majority of the cast also changed with only Cyril Smith continuing in his role as Emma Hornett's husband, Henry. As well as making the authors of the play rich, *Sailor, Beware!* also brought monetary security to Peggy for the first time in her life. Sensible as ever, it was her sudden upsurge in finances that allowed Peggy to ultimately invest in two homes: a large bungalow in her native Leigh-on-Sea and a home in central London.

Long before this date Peggy had been reading various plays in preparation for *Sailor, Beware!* ending, but admitted that she found it difficult to find something suitable for her second appearance in the West End. In the meantime the success of *Sailor, Beware!* also resulted in a feature film version being produced with Peggy in the starring role. Released in Britain on 4th September 1956, it was one of the most popular films of the year. Although Peggy once again played Emma Hornett, the screen version saw many changes to the cast including popular 1950s leading lady Shirley Eaton playing Emma's daughter, Shirley. Other starring roles were taken on by Ronald Lewis (as Albert Tufnell), Gordon Jackson (as Carnoustie Bligh), Cyril Smith (as Henry Hornett), Thora Hird (as Mrs Lack) and a scene-stealing Esma Cannon (as Edie Hornett). It stands as a lasting example of Peggy at her very best.

Without question Peggy made the role of Emma Hornett her own. Interestingly, despite its huge success in the 1950s, the play has only occasionally been revived and as a result very few actresses have taken on the role of the formidable mother-in-law. Arguably it is hard to imagine any other actress having anywhere near the same impact in a role that was so quintessentially 'Peggy Mount'. After the play's successful run in the West End, the role of Mrs Hornett was taken on by Amelia Bayntun, a member of the Joan Littlewood company and later a character player in several *Carry On* films. Over thirty years later, in 1994, Anna Karen, best known as Olive in the television sitcom *On the Buses*, 'sailed through the role of the family battleaxe' in a small production of the play on the Isle of Man; and Kathy Staff and Jane Freeman (familiar for their roles in *Last of the Summer Wine*) toured with the play in 1992/93.[95] Veteran actress Kathleen Harrison starred in the sequel, *Watch It, Sailor*, on stage in 1960-61 and also in the film version but generally speaking the role has remained Peggy's throughout the past sixty years. She would sum up the immense impact of the play on her life and career in 1996 by saying, 'Emma Hornett will always be my favourite part – because she gave me everything I ever wanted in the world.'[96]

In the spring of 1958, within months of closing in *Sailor, Beware!*, Peggy played Lady Bracknell in *The Importance of Being Earnest* at the Salisbury Playhouse, directed by Oliver Gordon. The appearance was widely regarded as a 'thank you' to Reginald Salberg, the general manager of the theatre, and his brother George who had both supported Peggy with work during her long years in repertory. Never one to forget her roots, or those who had helped her along the path to stardom, Peggy was only too pleased to take on the celebrated role in Oscar Wilde's popular play and to help the Salberg brothers in the process. Despite the vast difference in characterisations Peggy coped well with the role and managed to 'stay in character' and revealed a 'kindlier and more human *grande dame* than is generally seen'.[97]

In the same year she would star on television in *Arsenic and Old Lace*, produced by Bernard Braden, alongside Dave King, David Kossoff, Dorothy Dewhurst and Michael Bentine. In her role as Aunt Abby she received mixed reviews with one critic writing: 'Peggy Mount emerged as too strong a character to be suited for the part of a gently twittering murderess,'[98] while *The Birmingham Post* felt her performance was 'very robust'.[99]

By the late 1950s television was a fairly well-established medium although Peggy's small-screen appearances had been limited. Her long run at the Strand meant that she was unavailable for television work, and once her time as Emma

Hornett was up she was extremely conscious of choosing the right roles to maintain critical and personal success. In later life Peggy revealed she was 'offered a fortune to advertise things' but turned them down because she was 'interested in becoming an actress of note rather than an actress who made money'.[100] Once free from her long run on stage, Peggy continued to pursue roles on the small screen.

Her 1958 portrayal of Mamma Decomano in Peter Draper's play *The Visit to Paradise Buildings* was her first dramatic role on television and brought with it favourable reviews. Cruel and insensitive, Mamma Decomano is desperate to marry off her shy and diffident daughter (played by Margot van der Burgh) to an equally unpleasant shopkeeper played by Bill Nagy. The production also saw Peggy work alongside Barbara Lott, who later achieved national fame in the 1980s as Ronnie Corbett's mother in television's *Sorry!*[101]

For Peggy, television fame came later in 1958 and resulted in her achieving small-screen stardom. Her role in *The Larkins*, written by Fred Robinson and produced by Associated Television, was extremely well received and the production was regarded as 'undoubtedly one of the best comedy scripts on television'. Based on constant battles between Alf Larkins (played by David Kossoff) and his 'raucous' wife Ada (played by Peggy), it was a role for which she was perfectly suited. Critics regarded the character of Ada as a lovable 'tartar' and Peggy played the part with 'remarkable audacity'.[102]

Speaking of Peggy's involvement in the series, the show's first producer, Bill Ward, revealed she was apprehensive about taking on television work and the role which made her a small-screen star:

> She was in *Arsenic and Old Lace* when we approached her. She
> hadn't done any television, and felt wary about it, especially after the
> tremendous success of *Sailor, Beware!* That's why she only
> committed herself to an initial series of six, and wanted to satisfy
> herself about the scripts of any subsequent series. David Kossoff
> welcomed the chance, since he felt he was being typecast either as a
> cockney or continental.

Ward agreed that Peggy was 'a natural' for the part.[103] In
1996 Peggy would reveal she initially turned down the role of
Mrs Larkins because she did not want to be typecast, but
conceded: 'Then I read it and it was so wonderfully written I
couldn't resist.'[104]

Speaking about the part Peggy would admit, 'Ada isn't just
a Cockney wife. My years in repertory took me to theatrical
digs all over the country. There are Adas to the north, south,
east and west.'[105] The overwhelming success of the series led to
it being compared to the hit American series *I Love Lucy*
(starring Lucille Ball and Desi Arnaz) and the teamwork
between Mount and Kossoff was suitably praised by critics.

The series itself focused on the day-to-day antics of Ada and
her henpecked husband, their adult son Eddie (played by Shaun
O'Riordan), daughter Joyce (Ruth Trouncer) and son-in-law
Jeff (played by Canadian actor Ronan O'Casey), all living
together at 66 Sycamore Street. The cast was completed with the
presence of nosy neighbour Hetty Prout (Barbara Mitchell), her
husband Sam (George Roderick) and their daughter Myrtle
(Hilary Bamberger). When the series returned for a further two
series in 1963 and 1964 Ada and Alf Larkins had moved out of
their home (which had been demolished under a compulsory
purchase order) and were running a greasy-spoon café which
included bed-and-breakfast accommodation. Radio star Hugh

Paddick was called upon to play Osbert Rigby Soames, their 'toff' resident lodger, for a further fifteen episodes.

Performed and filmed in front of a live audience – and Peggy would concede 'You cannot do situation comedy without an audience'[106] – the popular sitcom ultimately ran for six series and forty episodes and secured Peggy's place in British national life.[107] The success of the programme even led to a well-received film version, titled *Inn For Trouble* (released in 1960), with Peggy and David in starring roles now running a country pub. Featuring a host of well-known faces, including Leslie Phillips, Charles Hawtrey and Irene Handl, the film was very much another chance for Peggy to shine on the big screen, proving that her talents were by no means limited to stage and television.

An earlier film appearance as writer Flora Ransom in *The Naked Truth* saw Peggy co-starring with Terry-Thomas (with whom she had previously worked in panto – see page 24) and Peter Sellers. Directed by Mario Zampi and written by Michael Pertwee, the amusing black comedy was released in December 1957 and centred upon the antics of magazine publisher Nigel Dennis (played by Dennis Price) as he attempted to blackmail various high-profile figures (including Peggy's character), and their subsequent attempts to murder him – both individually and later as a group. Peggy's character (assisted by her timid daughter Ethel, admirably played by future *Carry On* star Joan Sims) was quite different to her other on-screen performances, demonstrating a versatility which is often overlooked. With star billing just below Thomas and Sellers (and above Shirley Eaton who had already made almost a dozen film appearances by the age of twenty) it was another significant appearance in

Peggy's career, and regular repeats of the film have ensured it remains one of her best-known screen roles.

It was not until February 1959 that Peggy would take on another major stage role (this time opening at the Grand Theatre, Leeds) when she was cast opposite the iconic Margaret Rutherford in the H. M. Tennent production of *Farewell, Farewell, Eugene*, an adaptation by Rodney Ackland of an American play written by John Vari. Directed by William Chappell, the 'lightweight' comedy centred on two eccentric sisters who paint and write the verses of Christmas cards in order to save enough money to visit a relative who is a diamond prospector in Africa. Set in a house in Fulham in 1905, the play saw Peggy playing Florence Povis, 'a dominating puritan who was jilted in her youth' to Margaret Rutherford's Minerva Goody, 'a feather-brained widow'. Also among the cast was Avril Elgar, giving a fine performance as the sisters' niece who falls in love with a 'rough-spoken Irishman' played by Patrick McAlinney.

Proving once again that she could be far more than a battleaxe, Peggy, according to one review, brought 'boundless energy' to her very serious character of the Edwardian sister,[108] while Rutherford at the age of sixty-seven 'still has the heart of a young girl bursting to have fun' as she pranced about the stage 'like an insecure bell-tent in a breeze'.[109] Generally speaking it was Rutherford who received the best reviews and while she was regarded as 'brilliant' some felt that although Peggy 'touchingly' caught the pathos of the role she was still a little too loud and 'did not make the most of the comedy'.[110]

Despite a slightly mixed reception from critics and audiences alike, the teaming of two 'star' names in the form of

Rutherford and Mount saw the play transfer to the Garrick Theatre in London at the beginning of June 1959. An addition to the cast was future *Coronation Street* actor Philip Lowrie who later recalled how Peggy would bring in 'a selection of shrimps and crabs to share each week with the cast'. Lowrie would also remember how Peggy disapproved of Rutherford gaining 'cheap' laughs through her 'raucous' rendition of 'Knees Up Mother Brown', in which she revealed her bloomers to the audience.[111]

Peggy's work with Dame Margaret Rutherford inevitably led to comparisons between the two actresses. As the years passed, rightly or wrongly, they were increasingly associated with each other despite their vastly different appearances, personas and careers. With the exception of Madame Arcati in *Blithe Spirit* (famously immortalised by Rutherford on screen in 1945) their roles were invariably very different. Margaret Rutherford, despite a hugely successful career on stage and an Oscar-winning role as the Duchess of Brighton in *The V.I.P.s* in 1963, would become fixed in the minds of the general public as a slightly comedic version of Agatha Christie's famous amateur sleuth, Miss Marple, in four film adaptations, while Peggy would be forever remembered for her battleaxe roles on the small screen.

The differences between the two actresses were not only professional. Actress Damaris Hayman was a close personal friend to Rutherford for many years and confirms that Peggy and Margaret 'were not remotely friends'. Despite co-starring together for more than eight months, the connection between the two ladies was 'an entirely professional relationship' as Hayman recalls:

I don't think they liked each other very much… They were just fairly incompatible. Mount had made that crashing success in *Sailor, Beware!* having been, as far as I'm aware, in provincial rep up until then; Margaret, though she started late, got almost straight into the West End and stayed there *and* did films. I think the film version of *Sailor, Beware!* fell without trace.

During the run of *Farewell, Farewell, Eugene*, Damaris remembers being invited to a barbeque party Margaret Rutherford held for the cast of *Summer of the Seventeenth Doll* and clearly recalls that 'Peggy certainly wasn't asked to that.' The comparison between the two actresses is something that baffles Damaris, who also worked with Peggy on television in *Winning Widows*. In her late eighties, forthright and honest in her opinions, she would admit:

I can't think why she should be compared to Margaret! They couldn't have been more different if they'd tried. I mean Margaret was warm and loving; eccentric yes, but what's wrong with that? It's the glory of the English character.[112]

* * *

By now Peggy was extremely well known to the public at large. Fame inevitably brought with it a certain amount of negative publicity to which Peggy was never afraid to object. In 1960 she even went so far as to write an open letter to 'deny certain statements recently reported in the daily press':

At no time during my performance at 'The Night of 100 Stars' did I make any reference to 'Joie de Vivre', and at no time was it suggested that I refer to 'My Fair Lady' or the critics. I am deeply disturbed at the number of shows that have failed recently, and would certainly never dream of treating this subject in a light manner.

Thanking you for giving me this opportunity of making this clear
to my fellow professionals.
Yours sincerely,
Peggy Mount
40B Lexham Gardens, W.8
Administrator

Public recognition was something Peggy had to learn to
cope with. For her it was very much a double-edged sword, for
although she was more than happy to greet fans to sign auto-
graphs at the stage door following a performance, she disliked
being recognised at other times. The idea of being stopped by
fans in the street was something she certainly did not relish.

Actress Georgina Moon first got to know Peggy on stage in
the early 1970s during a long tour of *Fiddler's Three* and later
worked with her in television sitcom. She would recall how
Peggy tried to avoid public exposure:

Peggy would drive to Leeds for *You're Only Young Twice* because she
preferred not to be on the train. The public always wanted to talk to
her – and touch her – and I think after a while it became a little much.
She would drive because of that! She was always very kind to the
public but they really wanted to poke and prod her a bit. They always
wanted to give her a cuddle and put their arms around her.[113]

In private, even with close friends, Peggy was by no means
tactile; and, given her loveless upbringing, this is perhaps not
surprising. The idea of being 'cuddled' by strangers was totally
abhorrent to her.

As late as 1979, after more than two decades of stardom, it
was noted by journalist Peter McGarry who interviewed Peggy
that she continued to shy away from the attention of the
general public, even requesting that they change places in the
coffee bar where they had met with Peggy complaining,

'People keep looking at me.' On the same occasion she was approached by an autograph hunter and Peter witnessed first-hand that, while Peggy obliged 'graciously', she said very little.[114] While Peggy delighted in seeing her name in lights, away from the theatre she quite simply preferred to stay out of the limelight.

John Holmes, who met both Peggy and her sister Nancy, confirms her natural shyness and also her interest in others:

> The only conversation I had with Peggy was in Nottingham in the 1970s... when she played Mrs Malaprop in Sheridan's *The Rivals*. I was working at BBC Radio Nottingham at that time, and she came into our reception area to be interviewed by Dennis McCarthy. She was one of those elite bunch of personalities you think are lifelong friends even though, up until that moment, you've never met them. I greeted her, told her I went to Westleigh School and how proud I was of her success. She avoided talking about herself, just saying that she used to enjoy listening to the children playing in the playground. She then added something unexpected and something I'll never forget. Remember at the time she was one of the most well-known faces in Britain; 'Isn't it wonderful how well the Lloyd brothers are doing. I used to watch them as boys playing tennis in the middle of the road on Elmsleigh Drive and now look how well they've done!'[115]

4

A star is born

TO THE PUBLIC AT LARGE Peggy was now a television star – a fixture in millions of people's homes thanks to her role as Ada Larkins. On stage her career continued to blossom and in the early 1960s a variety of roles resulted in deep personal and professional happiness.

When Peggy joined the Old Vic for their 1960-61 season she was in the company of more than sixty actors, some working on tour and some performing at the Old Vic in the Waterloo Road. It was a star-studded company with names including Judith Anderson, Barbara Jefford, Joss Ackland, Tommy Steele and Judi Dench.

Peggy had hankered after good Shakespearean roles for years and made no secret of her desire to pursue serious work on stage. Once she had become an established star of the West

End she was eager to play Katherine of Aragon in *Henry VIII*, Maria in *Twelfth Night* or Constance in *King John*. Her greatest ambition was to take on the role of the Nurse in *Romeo and Juliet*, admitting as early as 1955 that it was her dream to work alongside her 'idol', Laurence Olivier. Following her success as Emma Hornett, one insightful critic even felt that she was a strong enough actress to play Lady Macbeth, although it was a role that never appealed to Peggy.

After admitting later, 'I had been offered every tough old lady that there ever was and I turned it all down,' a telephone call from Michael Benthall who ran the Old Vic resulted in Peggy's yearnings becoming a reality. Before he had a chance to offer Peggy the role of the Nurse in *Romeo and Juliet* she had already said 'Yes please,' to which Michael replied: 'Ooh, that's quick!' Candidly, Peggy replied, 'But you're an answer to prayer,' to which Michael responded, 'I've been called a lot of things in my time – but never an answer to prayer.'[116]

Almost sixty years after her appearance in Franco Zeffirelli's production of *Romeo and Juliet*, two of Peggy's co-stars would share their memories of Peggy at that time. Dame Judi Dench was at the very beginning of her illustrious career when she played Juliet in the production and would recall:

> During the run of *Romeo and Juliet*, I have to say that my concentration was taken up playing 'Juliet'. I do remember that Peggy Mount was wonderful as the Nurse. There was a scene, having just seen Tybalt's ghost, where I had to fall backwards into her arms. Having bruised my ribs (although I cannot now remember how), this was absolute agony every night. One other story I remember is when she invited me to have dinner with her and some friends at Le Caprice, and I managed to spill gazpacho all down her white stole. I was probably never invited again![117]

As Eira Griffiths would tell the author, Peggy had great admiration for Judi Dench, even at this early stage of the future Dame's career. It is possible she could see the spark that would enable Dench to become one of the greatest actors of her generation. Yet Peggy always had 'great respect for actors who respected their audiences and who gave to them a reality to which they could respond' and at this Judi Dench was already well adept.[118]

Another of Peggy's young colleagues at the Old Vic was Sir Tom Courtenay, who at the start of his long and successful career featured briefly in the production. Interestingly, two decades would pass before Peggy would take on further substantial Shakespearean roles. Although she did receive some good reviews for her role as the Nurse, with *The Scotsman* regarding it as a 'restrained and subtle performance', Sir Tom's memories shed some light on the possible reasoning behind Peggy's avoidance of the famous bard's work:

> I walked on in Zeffirelli's production of *Romeo and Juliet* in which Peggy played the Nurse. I recall that in a rave review of the production by Kenneth Tynan, Peggy was the only member of the cast to be excepted from the approval Tynan was scattering around. He went so far as to say everything about the production was good except for Peggy. I remember reading this and thinking how cruel and unnecessary this was. Why couldn't he have simply not mentioned her? It must have caused her pain. And in fact her performance was fine, I think, and in no way harmful to the evening's success. Tynan was very influential at that time. I thought he was cruel to Peggy when he needn't have been.[119]

Peggy was very much at home with the company. She was a team worker who kept her feet firmly on the ground and relied upon her colleagues, saying at the time, 'I am a producer's artist. I cannot work alone… My repertory years taught me a vital lesson. I cannot be brilliant alone: I must have a good part, good colleagues and a good director. As an actress, once you think you're marvellous, you've had it.' [120]

In the winter of 1960 Peggy played Mrs Hardcastle at the Old Vic in *She Stoops to Conquer* with Tommy Steele, Judi Dench, Ann Bell and Barbara Leigh-Hunt. This high-profile appearance gained much publicity and there were numerous press photographs of a toothy, beaming Peggy and an equally beaming Tommy Steele in many newspapers.

Despite still being in his early twenties, Tommy Steele's singing and acting career was already well established by this point; yet he remained grateful for the kindness of his older co-star, as he would recollect in 2017:

Peggy Mount was a 'wonderful everything'. Perhaps a small memorable moment might give you some idea of how kind she was. There we were on the first day of rehearsal for *She Stoops*. Was I nervous? No… petrified of course! But I had decided that I might use a northern accent for the part to cover up what I knew would be a shortcoming in my performance at such a place as the Old Vic. But how would the other actors react? I yelled my first line: 'Ey oop, by gum,' sort of thing. A silence fell on the room. Then came the Peggy boom: 'Aye, right lad.' The room roared with laughter and thanks to her… I was *in*!! [121]

Thankfully Peggy managed to cast off the shadow of *Sailor, Beware!* for this well-publicised performance. *The London Illustrated News* wrote of her piece: 'The bullying Mrs Hardcastle… has a fierce coyness that Peggy Mount manages with enjoyment. The woman might have been just Emma Hornett in 18th century dress, but Miss Mount is more than that.' [122]

Further success followed. Underneath the headline 'Peggy Mount domineers again' she received outstanding reviews for her role in *All Things Bright and Beautiful* at the Royal, Bristol (for the Bristol Old Vic Company). The play, written by Keith Waterhouse and Willis Hall, was described as: 'An exuberant and racy comedy about life in a North Country town… dealing with an earthy family whose members are either light-fingered or plumb lazy and whose strident "boss" is a mobile fortress of a woman who, when not chastising her youngest child, is yearning for the flowers and lawns of the long-promised home of a housing estate.' Naturally 'the boss' was played by Peggy with critics regarding the part as 'tailor made' for her. She gave a staggering performance, and praise for her 'wildly funny' role was fulsome: 'One can think of few actresses in the British theatre today who know how to handle this sort of leather-voiced comedy so well.' Supported by many future stars of television including Diana Hoddinott (playing Peggy's daughter), Thelma Barlow, Keith Barron, Paul Eddington, Christopher Benjamin and Milton Johns, Peggy was certainly in good company.[123]

All Things Bright and Beautiful was Diana Hoddinott's second-ever professional acting job. Over fifty years later she would remember Peggy's extreme kindness towards her, her admiration for Bruce Forsyth and Peggy's one piece of advice: 'that I shouldn't let anyone walk into my dressing room'.[124]

Thelma Barlow, who would go on to achieve iconic television success as Mavis Riley/Wilton in *Coronation Street*, would recall Peggy as a 'good team member' who 'joined an established repertory company and fitted in well'. At Christmas time Thelma remembered that Peggy bought 'the ladies of the cast red woollen knee-length knickers. Very welcome too. I am sure she enjoyed watching us open them. Goodness knows what she gave the men.'[125]

When the play transferred to London, Peggy was pleased to make a return to the West End. A change of cast saw the appearance of Jack Smethurst, who would later achieve television success in the 1970s sitcom *Love Thy Neighbour*. In 2017, at the age of eighty-five, Jack would recall his memories of Peggy to the author. He would remember Peggy as a 'very nice and motherly person' who despite her 'booming voice' was fundamentally 'a very private, gentle soul'. As the star of the play Jack regarded Peggy as 'the boss – obviously' but was always delighted to see her in later years, notably in the 1990s when Peggy came to see him on stage.[126]

The role of Queenie Hesseltine was evidently very much Peggy's and *The Tatler* commented that 'Miss Peggy Mount, as Ma Hesseltine, has her own mellow bellow which ranges from a blast to a yell.'[127] Although it was Dame Thora Hird who ultimately played Queenie on television in 1964, the role was one of Peggy's finest and one to which she would return over a decade later in her home town and on tour where her appearance was said to 'dominate the stage'.

In 1962 Peggy was a special guest at the *Daily Mirror* Award Show where she was presented with the award for Best Comedienne for her work in the television series *Winning Widows*, which ran for thirteen episodes over two series, co-starring Avice Landon and featuring David Stoll, an actor familiar to Peggy from her rep days. The star-studded event was attended by a host of big names including Bruce Forsyth, Margaret Lockwood, Hattie Jacques, Violet Carson, Isobel Barnett, and

Cliff Richard and the Shadows. In accepting the award Peggy paid tribute to scriptwriters Sid Green and Dick Hills, who penned the series about two thrice-widowed sisters who decide to move in together to cut down on costs. Peggy was cast as 'a raging battleaxe' with Landon as a 'trembling romantic sort', ably supported by the guest appearances of numerous leading players including Bernard Cribbins, Ronnie Stevens and Davy Kaye.[128] It was yet another string to Peggy's ever increasing bow.

* * *

The continued success of Peggy's career and rise to stardom was handled in a characteristically rational manner. While thrilled at her achievements, she was also well aware of the fickle nature of the acting profession. From the onset of stardom, Peggy clearly disliked 'playing' to the press – with whom she had frequent encounters. In 1996, she would recall having to jump into a freezing cold swimming pool for publicity photographs. It was a 'stunt' guaranteed to be disliked by Peggy. Another bugbear for her was being made to 'play to type' by the press. Actor Mark Curry would remember how Peggy talked about her three years *in Sailor, Beware!* in the West End, and described 'how she chose a really glamorous dress to wear for the press and publicity launch but was made to wear an apron and hairnet from the show instead!'[129]

Financial rewards were also handled sensibly – as shown by Peggy's changes of address. In 1954 Peggy was living at Flat 7, 97 Linden Gardens in Bayswater. Four years later she had moved to 40B Lexham Gardens in South Kensington; and a further two years after this, having achieved a degree of financial security for the first time in her life, she had moved to 44 Montagu Mansions in Crawford Street, W1. By 1967 she had moved to 33 Montagu Mansions, where she would remain for many years. In due course Peggy would also buy a large bungalow in her home town, which remained a beloved bolt-hole for decades, allowing her to escape London life. It was all a far cry from the numerous residences she had stayed in prior to achieving stardom, which included a variety of guest houses and even the flat above the Candy Shop in Malden Road, Colchester, where she had lived in 1953.

Peggy became increasingly wise to the nature of show business and avoided being roped into gimmicks, and was resolute in not becoming a 'celebrity'. Throughout her career she remained convinced that every new job would be her last, even after she had become well established as one of the country's best-known actresses. As a result of this, and perhaps because of her deprived upbringing, she was also careful with money – to the point of being frugal. Writer Pam Valentine would recall that any food left on set from a café scene during the filming of Peggy's later television series *You're Only Young Twice* would be collected by Peggy who would tell her co-star Pat Coombs, 'We'll have those, Patty, for the drive home.' Pam admits that Peggy was very much of the old-school way of thinking: 'It's the old actor thing of, "I may never work again, I may never have another meal." ' [130]

Actor John Standing, who became friends with Peggy, remembers her as a 'very, very gentle, quiet woman, very unflash. Very unpretentious. She was the reverse of everything she was cast in as an actress. Totally charming.' He admits the ups and downs of the business are a constant pressure felt by most thespians and Peggy was not immune to such demands:

Actors are the most vulnerable creatures ever – he has no will of his own. He has to learn somebody else's lines, move where he is told to by the director, be there on time, say what you have to and get off. That's really the truth of it all, whatever aspect of our job we are doing.[131]

Peggy's continued resolve not to become typecast led to her turning down many roles – and a fortune in earnings in the process. The sacrifice did not go unnoticed. When she was cast to play Agrippa opposite David Tomlinson's Nero in a Sewell Stokes comedy, *Mother's Boy*, it was duly noted that she saw the 'danger' of being typecast but her long years in repertory had provided her with 'a wealth of experience from which she is determined to benefit'. Peggy's lean years were also praised in the press: 'Acting is her life; she practically starved to follow her career.'[132] The chance to work with Tomlinson, now perhaps best remembered for his work in Disney films such as *Mary Poppins* (1964) and *Bedknobs and Broomsticks* (1971), appealed to Peggy but the play itself, slated as 'an orgy of boredom', was not well received with one critic writing: 'A sad evening at the Globe Theatre. Sad and frustrating to see such a waste of talent – David Tomlinson, Peggy Mount and Ann Bell – struggling to get laughs in one of the unhappiest, unfunniest farces I've ever seen.'[133]

Amid an array of stage roles Peggy also found time to make another film appearance, co-starring with the redoubtable Robert Morley and Harry H. Corbett, in the 1963 comedy *Ladies Who Do*, again written by Michael Pertwee. As cleaning lady Mrs Cragg, Peggy was playing very much to 'type' as the char who inadvertently profits on the stock market via rubbish collected from office waste-paper baskets. For fans of British comedy, *Ladies Who Do* is something of a treasure, featuring some of the best-loved actors of the era including Dandy Nichols, Miriam Karlin, Ron Moody, Avril Elgar, Jon Pertwee and Cardew Robinson. The film makes for enjoyable watching with Peggy once again showing off her confidence and skill as a film actress.

Over the next few years Peggy would go on to star in three more feature films. She worked again with Robert Morley on two further occasions in *Hotel Paradiso* and *Finders Keepers* (a follow-on from Cliff Richard's *Summer Holiday*), while her role as Mrs Myra Gantry in the slightly bizarre *One Way Pendulum* (a film version of the popular stage play) was limited but brought with it the kudos of 'guest' billing.

Although Peggy's film appearances were relatively few, she would look back with pleasure on the opportunity to work with one of her favourite stars: Sir Alec Guinness in *Hotel Paradiso*. Thirty years after this appearance Peggy would recount one of her famous stories from the set to her young colleague, Mark Curry:

> She told me about her first day on set in the film *Hotel Paradiso*, when she had to take a hatpin and stick it into the behind of Alec Guinness. In a rehearsal she had held back, not wanting to hurt him; and Alec said, pompously, 'Are you going to do it with more feeling?' to which Peggy responded, 'If you want this up your arse then you're welcome,' and then apparently on the 'take', she *certainly* gave it more feeling! [134]

Peggy admitted in her 1996 *Desert Island Discs* interview that she and Guinness both 'fell about with laughter' following the incident and that she was shocked to find out later that 'he was more afraid of me than I was of him'. [135] In 1973, along with many other famous faces including Jack Watling, Anthony Quayle, Dorothy Tutin, Gordon Jackson and Patricia Hayes, she attended the Gallery First Nighters Club special dinner in honour of Sir Alec; and in 1996, by which time they were both in their eighties, Peggy would admit that she was 'absolutely in awe' of her contemporary.[136]

Despite its all-star cast, including Italian beauty Gina Lollobrigida, the film received mixed reviews as indeed did Peggy's other screen appearances at the time. It was perhaps no surprise, then, that she chose to concentrate on work in the theatre where – after almost a decade as a star actress – her reputation was secure.

Back in the theatre *The Beaver Coat* was considered to be 'another excellent vehicle' for Peggy and she received excellent reviews for her role as a 'boisterously cunning local housewife'. *The Stage* wrote: 'Peggy Mount – under the cloak of apparent honesty – is getting away with anything from petty poaching to the stealing of a valuable fur coat. Miss Mount, heavy-handed and light-fingered, crookedly jovial, domineering and crafty, twists everyone, including her audience, around her little finger.'[137] She would repeat the role of Mrs Wolff in Gerhart Hauptmann's satirical play on several occasions. In addition there were other roles on stage, including co-starring with Rosamond Burne in *What About Stanley?* a new farce by Betty Paul and Peter Lambda at the Alexandra Theatre, Birmingham, where once again her comedic talents were said to have lifted the play.

5

Dragon and beyond

'A top rate comedienne'

AFTER TWO YEARS' ABSENCE from a regular role on the small screen, in 1966 Peggy was thrilled to be back on television, co-starring with Sid James, in the first of three series of the situation comedy *George and the Dragon*. She admitted to being 'excited' at the prospect of working with James, whom she had 'long admired' (both had featured in the 1956 film *Dry Rot* although Peggy admitted their 'paths never really crossed' during the course of that production). The series had Peggy on familiar ground since it was produced by Alan Tarrant (who had also produced *The Larkins* from series three onwards), and directed by Shaun O'Riordan, who had played Peggy's son in the same series.

Written by Vince Powell and Harry Driver, *George and the Dragon* saw Peggy playing cook/housekeeper Gabrielle Dragon, a widow with a no-nonsense attitude employed by Colonel Maynard, played by the affable John Le Mesurier (who within a few short years became a television star in *Dad's Army*). Clashing with Sid James's character, the lecherous chauffeur and handyman George Russell, and occasionally with Ralph, the unwashed gardener (played by Keith Marsh), Gabrielle Dragon was the kind of strong, assertive woman with which Peggy was now synonymous.

In a rare interview at the time Peggy would reveal her feelings about working with Sid James – one of the country's biggest stars thanks to his work in the *Carry On* films and, earlier, on television with Tony Hancock:

> People always think I'm three times bigger than I really am because I'm usually cast against smaller men… but Sid and I are evenly matched. We're about the same weight – I don't mean physically but in terms of strength of voice and the characters with whom we are associated in the viewers' minds.
>
> I had often thought my style and Sid's would blend perfectly, and so it is proving… Sid and I are having a great time.
>
> Sid has the one thing all good comedians must have. He is lovable. You can't help loving Sid, no matter what character he's playing. He plays a rogue but you *still* love him.

Also featured heavily in the same interview was Peggy's lifelong insecurity about her looks and weight. Despite being over fifty and well-established as a star actress Peggy remained conscious of her appearance saying:

> I'd like to be slim, dark, beautiful with a high pitched voice. I squirm when I see myself on screen. That big fat thing, great big chin, all gums and teeth and a booming voice. How could anyone ever laugh at that? I remember coming out of a private screening for me of the film *The Naked Truth* in fear and trembling because I seemed so

dreadful. Yet when I saw it with an audience I realised I was getting
as big a share of the laughs as the others.[138]

Peggy's personal anxieties, however, were certainly lessened
by her sheer delight in working with Sid James, and the feeling
was mutual. In 2017 Sid's daughter Susan would remember
that the James family felt it was one of his best television series
and that Peggy herself was 'a delight'.[139] Like Peggy, Sid James
was well known for his absolute professionalism and was
always keen to stick to the script. He disliked working with
actors who ad-libbed, and like any skilled thespian thoroughly
appreciated his colleagues knowing their lines. In this respect,
Peggy was his ideal co-star and theirs was a rare, near-perfect
professional partnership. In 1969 Sid would admit quite
simply: 'I liked working with Peggy – she is a great professional
and knows just what she is doing.'[140]

Given that both Peggy and Sid had previously starred in
highly successful small-screen productions, their being paired
together for their very own sitcom perhaps seemed inevitable
and the 'matching of the elongated walnut and the foghorn' was
immediately hailed a success. Peggy's portrayal of Gabrielle
Dragon was slightly more subtle than some of her previous
characterisations with one critic noting that she 'no longer
uses her foghorn voice like a distracted ship in a minefield. She
booms only occasionally and is the more effective for it.'[141]

At times, despite his long career in the business and in-
stantly recognisable face and persona, Peggy even dominated
the screen over her co-star – and guest stars, including the
formidable stage actress, Sonia Dresdel. One writer at the time
stated of Peggy: 'She is plain, large, loud and her comic sense
makes Sid James look like an amateur. This show, like other

good comedy shows, is ideal for the "guest appearances" and on Saturday it was Sonia Dresdel queening it over the servants and being predictably out-pointed by Peggy Mount.'[142]

The initial run of six episodes screened in the winter of 1966 proved highly popular, leading to a further two series being commissioned in 1967 and 1968. The on-screen chemistry between Mount and James was clear to see, and after fifty years the series still makes for delightful viewing. The character of Gabrielle Dragon, immaculately dressed and accessorised and also at times slightly vulnerable, was certainly far removed from Peggy's previous screen incarnations, and the series remains one of her finest.

After a spate of film appearances in the early 1960s, towards the end of the decade Peggy would take on the iconic role of the tyrannical Mrs Bumble in Carol Reed's *Oliver!* Thanks to constant repeats of the much-loved musical, Peggy's role of Harry Secombe's overbearing wife is perhaps her best-known big-screen appearance. The film was certainly the biggest commercial success of Peggy's film career, gaining eleven Oscar nominations (and six wins) and earning over $77 million at the box office. Filmed at Shepperton Studios in the summer of 1967, Peggy's appearance in the film was relatively brief, yet she was perfectly cast to appear alongside Welsh-born actor and singer (Sir) Harry Secombe playing the unforgettable, pompous beadle of the workhouse. Their appearance together led to further professional associations, with Peggy guest-starring in Harry's television series in 1968 and 1969. The pair (who died within months of each other) were clearly fond colleagues and always happy to encounter each other over the years at various show-business events.

The child star of the film was actor Mark Lester in the lead role of the orphaned Oliver Twist. As with many children, Peggy's slightly formidable appearance did not impact on Mark and, although just eight years old when he encountered Peggy, and therefore unable to recall any specific stories attached to her, he would remember her 'as being highly professional and a warm-hearted person'.[143]

Despite continuing to work as a professional actress for the next thirty years, *Oliver!* proved to be Peggy's final feature film. The big screen had undoubtedly not made the most of her talents, although she was perhaps too powerful a presence to be relegated to cameo roles in films and equally too difficult to cast in starring roles. Sensibly Peggy avoided appearing in any of the multitude of low-budget film comedies produced in Britain throughout the late 1960s and 1970s (which would have been unworthy of her talents), and unlike some of her contemporaries was not drawn to appear in any of the equally cheaply made horror flicks so popular at the time. Her handful of screen comedies, made between 1956 and 1964, survive as a lasting record of her formidable talent and unforgettable voice and on the whole have stood the test of time.

In the midst of Peggy's renewed television fame, a personal bereavement arose which must surely have been met with mixed feelings. Peggy's mother, Rose Mount, died following a stroke at Rochford General Hospital on 30th November 1968. Her death was registered by Nancy and she was recorded as the widow of Alfred Mount, 'a manager (provision merchants)'. Rose was eighty-four years old at the time of her death and passed on her longevity to both of her daughters. She had lived long enough to see Peggy become a star of stage, screen and television, yet her thoughts on her younger daughter's success are unrecorded. Likewise Peggy's reaction to her mother's death is also unknown. From Nancy Mount's 1993 BBC radio interview it is clear that Rose continued to perform as a singer, albeit locally, well into old age; but it appears that Peggy did not maintain contact with her only surviving parent, despite living in close proximity. In 1996 she would discuss, briefly, her relationship with Rose and the impact it had on her, saying that her mother's 'lovelessness' may have influenced her decision never to marry, while also conceding marriage may have meant a choice between love or her career. Never one to complain or wallow in self-pity, Peggy would go on to say of her relationship with her mother: 'I don't regret it. I'm not sour or bitter about it.' [144]

Despite knowing Peggy for decades Eira Griffiths admits that she never heard Peggy mention Rose, even in passing conversation: 'I don't think she ever spoke about her mother or Nancy... never. She was very much estranged from her family.' [145] Whether or not Peggy even attended her mother's funeral remains a mystery, although if she did it may have been the last time she would have faced direct contact with her only sibling. The death of Rose Mount ultimately severed Peggy's last link with her family and her unhappy childhood.

Despite her fame she remained fundamentally a shy person, who, like many actors, found confidence and an escape in the make-believe world of acting. By now in her fifties, Peggy remained single. She had placed her career above everything else and in doing so achieved professional success, national and international fame and gained financial security. Acting remained the great joy and passion of her life – and would remain so until the very end. It was surely no exaggeration when she once said: 'It's not like work really. I love it and, for me, acting will always come first.'[146]

* * *

Another television series following on from *George and the Dragon* saw Peggy back in the centre of the public domain and once again working alongside Shaun O'Riordan who both produced and directed *John Browne's Body*, a comedy thriller starring Peggy and her recent stage colleague, Naunton Wayne.[147] The series centred upon Peggy's character, respectable insurance broker Virginia Browne, inheriting a half share in her late brother's detective agency, with Naunton Wayne playing the other partner. Written by Rene Basilico, the seven-episode series saw the pair becoming involved with various unscrupulous characters, many of whom were associated with Virginia's equally unscrupulous brother.

Screened in the spring of 1969, the series received mixed reviews. The vastly different style of Mount and Wayne was noted, as too was their professionalism and ability to work well with somewhat limited material. While it is unlikely the series would have been long-lived, alas any chance of a second series was cut short by the death of Naunton Wayne in the following year at the age of sixty-nine.

Greater acclaim came in 1969 on stage in J. B. Priestley's *When We Are Married*. It was noted that Peggy received a standing ovation for her 'highly diverting role' as Clara Soppitt, 'the formidable dragon of a wife, one of the three who, with their husbands, had met to celebrate their silver weddings only to find that they had not been legally married'.[148] The following year, 1970 (after returning from Australia where she had been appearing on stage in *The Bandwagon*), Peggy opened at the Yvonne Arnaud Theatre in Guildford in another version of *When We Are Married*. This time the cast included many high-profile names including Renée Asherson, Freda Jackson, Hugh Lloyd, Fred Emney, Frank Thornton, William Moore (her old colleague in rep), Shirley Steedman and Claire Davenport.

When We Are Married was the first of several occasions when Peggy would work with theatrical producer Duncan C. Weldon. Although aware that Peggy could be 'tough', Duncan admitted that she never was with him and that they got on well, with Peggy remaining 'loyal' to him throughout the remainder of her career.[149]

At the end of the year the play had transferred to the Strand, the well-known scene of Peggy's first stage triumph some fifteen years earlier, with a slight change of cast. It was at the Strand that J. B. Priestley himself received bows from the cast members and applause from the audience as he watched the production. It was a touching and heartfelt tribute to the author of the long-running and successful play.

The 1970s proved to be a tumultuous decade. National strikes impacted on Peggy's everyday life and, on a more personal level, resulted in her speaking out on political matters. In 1971, when the profession decided not to join the protest strike over the Government's Industrial Relations Bill, Peggy was one of a number of actors to voice their opinions on the subject. Led by Vanessa Redgrave, more than 1,200 members of Equity, the actors' union, met at the Adelphi Theatre to vote on the matter with Peggy later agreeing with the majority vote (of five to one) against the strike. Along with Robert Morley, Tommy Steele, Jimmy Edwards and Sir John Clements, Peggy was thoroughly against the idea of action and admitted, 'I don't believe in strikes at all.'[150] Although not especially politically minded, Peggy was also among a group of actors, including Dame Peggy Ashcroft and Ian (later Sir Ian) McKellen, who went to 10 Downing Street in January 1971 to present signatures of thousands of working members of Equity in support of a letter written to the Prime Minister by members of the National Theatre Company.[151] Despite such upsets the decade provided Peggy with a flurry of work both on stage, where she continued to tour extensively throughout the country, and on television in a further two hit comedy series.

A lack of what she deemed to be worthy material – and her own ambitious desire to stay at the top of her game – had resulted in Peggy turning down a variety of television scripts over a period of several years. In 1971 she revealed: 'I've not had much faith in anything since *The Larkins*.' She had good reason to be cautious. Despite her string of professional successes, not all of Peggy's performances were hits. A television appearance with fellow veteran Deryck Guyler in 1973, for example, proved to be a one-off which sank without trace. *Quiet Waters*, a pilot for Thames Television, saw Peggy as the 'bellowing matron' in a home for retired officers with Guyler playing an ex-major. It was savaged in the press with one critic writing: 'Their material was so woeful that I could not even raise an embarrassed snigger as the cast strained its way through an almost non-existent plot.'[152] After a few years of declining regular television work, however, Peggy at last agreed to take on the role of Maggie Robinson in *Lollipop Loves Mr Mole,* with the hope of achieving another small-screen hit. She made no secret of her desire to maintain her reputation as a star actress, saying: 'I don't mind admitting that my nose will be put out of joint a bit if we don't get into the top ten ratings.'

A total of fourteen episodes of *Lollipop Loves Mr Mole* were produced, over two series, between 1971 and 1972, each written by Jimmy Perry especially for Peggy and Hugh Lloyd, who was cast as her husband Reg. Supported in each episode by Pat Coombs and Rex Garner (as Reg's brother and sister-in-law), the production also featured a range of guest actors including Bill Pertwee and Michael Knowles.

While playing to the strengths of the two main stars, *Lollipop Loves Mr Mole* (the title referred to the couple's pet names for each other and was abbreviated simply to *Lollipop* for the second series), Jimmy Perry (well known as the co-writer of such classics as *Dad's Army*, *It Ain't Half Hot Mum* and *Hi-De-Hi!*), later admitted Peggy's initial portrayal of Maggie Robinson left him shocked:

> The trouble came when, in the first week of rehearsal for *Lollipop*, she was playing the part in a very quiet way. I'd written it for an aggressive, dominant woman with a heart of gold, which made a wonderful contrast to the meek and mild Hugh Lloyd. When I tackled Peggy about it she said, 'Oh, I don't want to play aggressive, shouting women any more.'

Despite feeling that the series was 'rubbish' Jimmy was commissioned to write another by Bill Ward, head of light entertainment at ATV at the time, who was more than happy with the viewing figures of over 16 million.[153]

Almost inevitably Peggy's new role on television brought with it press attention, and she revealed in a *Daily Mirror* interview that she was well aware that she was now typecast as a 'dragon' – a label she hated but had used to name the boat she continued to enjoy during breaks from acting. Of her screen image, almost mirroring Jimmy Perry's sentiments, Peggy admitted: 'It's no good my trying to get away from it. I'm me. People expect me to shout and rave. They're disappointed if I don't. At first I underplayed the whole thing, because I gathered that's what they wanted me to do. But it wasn't right. It wasn't quite me.'[154] Having changed tactics, and providing more of the 'big voice', Peggy knew in which direction she would take the character, to the delight of the crew and ultimately the viewing public.

The character of Maggie, still blissfully in love with her diminutive, kind-hearted husband after ten years, was seen as protective rather than domineering and much of her time was spent trying to stop him being taken advantage of. In the first episode of the series the couple welcome Violet and Bruce Robinson (Coombs and Garner) into their Fulham home when they visit from South Africa, accompanied by six large cabin trunks. When the pair outstay their welcome Maggie becomes increasingly frustrated with their antics.

The teaming of Peggy and Hugh Lloyd was at the direct request of ATV. The pair had previously worked together on stage and their careers were both well established by the time they were cast as husband and wife. In his 2002 autobiography Hugh Lloyd would describe Pat Coombs as 'lovely' and a close personal friend, yet his summary of Peggy was less affectionate – and brief. He described his co-star as 'larger-than-life' and the 'queen' of 'formidable ladies'.[155] Although they would go on to appear together on television again in *It's Never Too Late*

(1984), it appears theirs was a purely professional relationship. Actress Damaris Hayman, who worked with Peggy on television in *Winning Widows* and also knew Hugh, believes that Peggy 'wouldn't have been his style at all'.[156]

Ian Masters, who toured with Peggy in *The Mating Game* and wrote *It's Never Too Late*, was close friends with Hugh Lloyd (who was best man for Ian when he married for a second time) and confirms that the relationship between Mount and Lloyd was not an easy one:

> Peggy was an interesting person: quite a mixture. Quite private in lots of ways; quite puritanical. If she thought someone was being not quite 'good', or she'd heard rumours they'd been naughty or were having affairs on tour or things like that, she was completely cold and she could completely snub people.
>
> Hugh Lloyd had a bad time with her during the rehearsals and he kept saying to me, 'I don't know what I've done,' and I said, 'Don't worry about it.' She used to get a bee in her bonnet that somebody had done something out of her puritanical sphere, as it were, and she would strangely go really off you... Poor Hugh was really upset because he didn't know what he'd done, but then she'd come round.[157]

With another television success under her belt, Peggy resumed her work on stage with a succession of celebrated appearances. For an actress now in her mid fifties her work rate was enviable, proving that as a star character actress she had far more professional longevity than many leading ladies who at such an age often struggle to secure decent parts.[158]

During this busy time in her professional life Peggy's persona impacted greatly on many of her colleagues, none more so than playwright Terence Frisby, best known as the author of the smash hit *There's a Girl in My Soup*, who admits that he 'adored' Peggy. His memories, kindly shared with the author in 2017, are worth recording in full:

I first met Peggy in 1969 when she was in a play of mine called *The Bandwagon*.

Robert Chetwyn wanted to cast her. He had already brilliantly directed a most successful play of mine, a worldwide hit, *There's a Girl in My Soup* (indeed, he had invented that wonderful title) and he thought a great deal of Peggy's work. One thing he was always fond of saying was that, though Peggy was known as a top-rate comedienne in this country (the archetypical mother-in-law after the performance that made her name in *Sailor, Beware!* and a regular performer as a working-class dragon), had she lived on the Continent, especially Germany, she would have been at some state theatre playing Mother Courage and other great roles. He was always happy to complain about her underuse and to castigate our National Theatre for not casting her in something substantial. After working with her I agreed with him. She had more to give than was ever sought, to my knowledge.

The Bandwagon was what I called a serious low comedy. So much of what we were then calling farce (Whitehall farces, Carry On films) was really low comedy. Only nobody was ever asked to take it seriously: face-pulling, overacting and scripts that insulted your intelligence. It seemed that one had to look back to Ben Jonson to see intelligent low comedy that had a point other than to create laughs. I could write another few pages trying to define what is low comedy, high comedy, satire, comedy of manners, or character as we say now, but shall spare you. Anyway, that was what I was trying to do and Robert, Michael Codron the producer and I had cast my play beautifully with actors who would be funny while never forsaking their humanity.

The play was about an eighteen-year-old girl who was heavily pregnant. She lived with her family, the Botterills, in a rent-controlled flat in New Cross. Overcrowded and penniless, this family consisted of Mum (Peggy), Dad (Ronald Radd), older sister Lorraine (Toni Palmer), her husband Bernard (Ron Pember) and their two little children, older brother Leslie (Ron Wellings) and the pregnant girl herself, Aurora (Denise Coffey). All of the women were pregnant and Aurora comes home to announce that she's about to have quintuplets. General horror. Where can they put everybody? What will they do?

However, the hospital have leaked the information to a big advertising agency and, before they can think, the family are overwhelmed by advertising people, lawyers and a TV news team (tipped off by the advertising people) trying to get them on the evening news after the advertising agency have signed Aurora up for large sums of money. Of course, the multiple pregnancies create utter confusion as the unborn quins are bought and sold at breathtaking speed. Brother Leslie is taken for the father-to-be and the TV news people move in to interview Aurora. As she is being interviewed on live TV she admits to the fact that she's not married, that she doesn't know the father's name ('He's a soldier,' she says helpfully) and that the loveless conception took place, mostly because of her sexual ignorance, in a back alley on a rainy November night, with the squaddie, who she'd just met.

'How did this happen?' asks the agonised interviewer.

'My friend, Sylve, told me it was safe standing up,' volunteers Aurora, and the programme is taken off the air. (This was the sixties, remember. TV still had some very strict rules, even the news broadcasts. We were only just coming out of all sorts of long-standing censorship constraints.)

The delicious irony of this is that I first wrote the play as a TV script and, due to bungling at the BBC, that line ensured that it was never shown. An autocratic, newly promoted executive, Gerald Savory, tried to ban the line against an agreement I already had with his predecessor. It ended up in the High Court. I won an action against the BBC, forbidding the play to be performed without it. The line had spawned the play originally in my mind and now it stopped it being shown.

Delighted, I adapted it for the stage, which had only recently rid itself of the Lord Chamberlain and official censorship. My intention, as is evident, was to contrast the low comic event of the conception of the quins and the lives of the family with the gloss, commercialisation and hypocrisy of the advertising industry. Ominously, it had a cast of seventeen, quite costly; I had spread myself after the success of *There's a Girl in My Soup*, to Michael Codron's dismay.

I trusted Robert with my play and tried not to clutter up rehearsals with my presence. But it was a premiere and I wanted to see that the text was right. We had work to do, especially on the ending. So on some days there I sat, while they rehearsed, making notes with a concentrated look on my face. After a run-through of the first act, during which I scowled relentlessly as I scribbled notes wondering where I could improve it, Robert took me aside.

'Look, Terry, do you think you could stay away as much as possible, only you completely unnerve Peggy. She's terrified of you and when you're there frowning and making notes she thinks they're for her and her concentration just goes.'

I was horrified, assured her through him that I loved her work and stayed away except for one other run-through when my appreciative chuckles were clearly heard by all the cast. That Peggy Mount, the famous gorgon, should be frightened of me seemed unbelievable.

The family were like a six-headed juggernaut, an unstoppable force down the middle of the play, headed by Peggy. They were wonderful and I loved them all jointly and individually. Denise Coffey, who played Aurora, won the Clarence Derwent Award for best supporting actress (the one awarded by Equity, the actors' award for actors. There wasn't one for leading actress. This was like an Olivier award would be today). She said to me afterwards, 'Supporting actress? Funny. I thought I was playing the lead.'

'So did I,' I answered. And so she was.

But her performance and the whole family rested on the great rock of Peggy as the mother. She was magnificent. There was a moment that summed her performance up and I don't think could have been done by any other actress I've ever seen. Aurora is going to lose a fortune if she doesn't marry the soldier, who she doesn't like and doesn't really know. Her father urges her to do as she wishes. They'll look after her. She turns to her mother, who is knitting for her own accidental and very late-in-life addition to the family.

'What shall I do, Mum?'

Peggy came to the end of a row and adjusted her knitting needles while we waited. She looked at her plain, rather dim daughter as the father said, 'Let her make up her own mind.'

Peggy's voice rumbled up from some subterranean place.

'Own mind, my arse. You marry him. Marry 'im, my girl. It's the best chance you'll get in this life. Make no mistake.'

It was so simple and she made it so powerful. It carried the wisdom of working-class, hard-working, practical women throughout the ages. I loved Peggy for that moment alone.

We were in the Mermaid Theatre and never got a transfer in spite of excellent notices, partly because of Michael's reservations on the costs. He told me that the owner of the Strand Theatre (now the Novello), where Peggy had had a three- or four-year run with *Sailor, Beware!*, her massive hit, said he would take us if we would beef up Peggy's part and make her louder. This crass judgement cut no ice with any of us so, theatreless, we died at the Mermaid after our scheduled three-month run was up. I went in one night and listened to the laughter resounding round the auditorium, soon to be silent. Ron Wellings said to me, 'If this is what it's like to be in a flop, I can't wait to be in a hit.' (He soon was: he did a year in *Soup* as Jimmy, the young boyfriend.) *The Bandwagon* went on to be very successful in Australia, with Peggy in it again and Robert directing, and all over the Continent, where it was bigger than *Soup* in some countries.

I next met her in 1979 at Birmingham Rep. I was playing the Tom Walls part in a revival of the most famous Aldwych farce, *Rookery Nook*. Peggy was playing Mrs Leverett, the housekeeper. We were scheduled to come in to the West End to Her Majesty's in the Haymarket. I had to play one of the opening scenes with her and couldn't get it right. I was also a bit overwhelmed about acting with her. I was threshing about trying things. In a break in rehearsal she said to me of my character, 'He's a charmer. He doesn't give a toss. Certainly not about a housekeeper. That's all there is to him. You can do it standing on your head.'

It relaxed me and set me right at once. She was no longer an actress, overwhelmed by what she thought was a disapproving author, but an older member of the company helping out a nervous colleague.

Peggy was excellent as Mrs Leverett, of course, no surprise there. There was one scene with Andrew Robertson playing the henpecked husband, the Robertson Hare part, that was sublime. The characters were both utterly misunderstanding the other and getting into a deeper and deeper muddle. We other members of the cast would gather in the wings to watch it night after night just to enjoy great farce acting (quite unhurried, thoughtful, measured, even slow, from both of them) and to listen to the deafening round of applause that concluded the scene each night. Peggy could not come into London with the show and the part was taken over by another famous comedienne. It was like a gaping hole where Peggy had been. The scene above barely got laughs and never a round. The show sputtered and closed in some weeks.[159]

* * *

In the summer of 1971 Peggy once again took on the role of Emma Hornett when Duncan C. Weldon and Paul Elliott presented *Sailor, Beware!* at the Ashcroft Theatre in Croydon. Teaming with her former television co-star Keith Marsh and also Gretchen Franklin, it was not the last time Peggy would resurrect the character since she went on to play her most famous harridan on radio a decade later.

Performing for the Royal Shakespeare Company for two weeks over Christmas 1971 in a musical version of *Alice in Wonderland* saw Peggy co-starring with Jack Hulbert (as the Caterpillar and the King of Hearts), Desmond Walter-Ellis (as the Mad Hatter) and Anthony Booth. It proved to be a poignant return to the Stratford stage, where twenty-five years earlier she had played the maid in J. B. Priestley's *Eden End* during her time with the Colchester repertory company.

Peggy was thrilled to feature in a play specifically designed for children. It had been two decades since her appearance as the Witch in the pantomime *Humpty Dumpty* and she admitted to relishing the responsiveness of a young audience. Playing both the Queen and the Duchess brought her particular joy, and she revealed: 'I wouldn't have played the Queen unless I could have played the Duchess as well, because the Duchess is a very funny character. I shall wear a false nose and be very ugly. The Queen's laughs are mostly in team work and business, but the Duchess has to get hers off her own bat, and that is always a challenge.' It was with some regret that Peggy revealed that her earlier LP recording of the Queen filled children with dread and fear (to the point where even children she knew became frightened of her!). As a result she deliberately attempted to 'take the sting out of the Queen, and make her a figure of fun'.[160] Children provided Peggy with a highly responsive audience, which she loved, and at the end of her career lively pantomime appearances would become a staple of her work. To assist her in preparing for panto Peggy called upon the advice of actor George Moon, who was a veteran of the genre. Years later she never forgot his kindness; and, following his death in 1981, his daughter, actress Georgina Moon, would recall how Peggy 'sent flowers to my Mamma… she was such a kind person and remembered the help George had given her in a note'.[161]

Her appearance in the West End in *There Goes the Bride* brought Peggy into contact with the renowned playwright Ray Cooney who would recall her in 2017 to the author:

> She was very much a team member, a big strong lady and highly professional which is what you want in these kinds of plays. I certainly never had a cross word with her and I never saw a cross word with any of the directors who worked with her… It was a lovely time.

Her comic timing came naturally to her, but she also took the notes. With some of these plays, especially mine, they are complicated. I would maybe be watching from the back of the theatre and she would take all the notes from the director and I might whisper something to the director and she would accept those. She was just a professional actress.

Because there wasn't a role for her in my plays I never worked with her again. The last time I saw her was when she did *Rookery Nook* but she continued working until the end.

She was a delightful lady to be with and a wonderful member of the company… not a battleaxe at all – she could put it on brilliantly. That's why everyone thought she was a battleaxe, because she would deliver. She was lovely.[162]

Peggy's role as Mrs Malaprop in *The Rivals* at the Belgrade Theatre in Coventry almost saw her returning to her repertory theatre roots. The production was directed by Warren Jenkins and included a short tour. One of Peggy's co-stars in *The Rivals* was Jeffrey Holland, who would achieve fame a decade later as Spike in the popular and long-running television comedy series *Hi-De-Hi!* Jeffrey would remember Peggy with affection as a 'lovely lady' who took him and his first wife Eleanor (who featured in *The Rivals* as a maid and, as a trained hairdresser, also looked after the wigs on the production) under her wing:

She sort of adopted us as surrogate children because she enjoyed company – she used to talk and tell us stories of what she'd done. It was quite an education really. She looked after us. In return we tried to do whatever she needed us to do for her.

Looking back on this 'wonderful time' Jeffrey would remember Peggy's black BMW ('it was posh – she was a star') and her 'lovely flat' in London to which he and Eleanor were invited. He was also well aware of Peggy's reputation:

> She could be a bit scary I must admit. She didn't suffer fools. Never
> mind gladly – she didn't suffer them at all! She had no time for idiots.
> We fitted the bill that she liked, thank goodness.[163]

Further tours in various plays around the country during the 1970s and even into the 1980s continued to be slightly reminiscent of her long years in rep. By now, however, she was able to enjoy a certain degree of luxury and take time to enjoy local surroundings with her colleagues. Georgina Moon, in the first major stage tour of her career, spent several months with Peggy and recalls: 'Peggy was absolutely delightful to be with and would find nice places to stay, and very often after the show we would go back to wherever she was staying. She was a great cook and a great knitter.' In addition to being a hospitable star actress, Peggy also enjoyed arranging outings for her colleagues including, as Georgina Moon recalls, a visit to the 'lovely little Georgian Theatre in Richmond where she arranged a wonderful tour for us all. She would do things like that – it was totally her.' Always happy to drive, Georgina remembers that Peggy had a succession of cars including 'a boxy BMW – which was not the kind of car you expected to see someone like Peggy in… She'd drive everywhere.'[164]

Occasionally Peggy's famous face played to her advantage. Eira Griffiths recalls Peggy getting lost in Birmingham's in-famous Spaghetti Junction and being escorted by the police who recognised her, and also going the wrong way down a one-way street. She also managed to attract the attention of the police, for the wrong reasons, whilst using a roundabout in Aberdeen. Whether Peggy's on-screen persona or her famous face saved her from receiving fines remains unknown but she was, as Eira remembers, nevertheless, grateful for police assistance.

In her seventies, by which time her failing eyesight was giving serious cause for concern, Peggy had more or less given up driving and so became a reluctant passenger. Designer Claudia Mayer would recall occasionally chauffeuring Peggy to and from the Thorndike Theatre in 1987 during their time together in *Party Piece* and remembers being 'so frightened to be driving a national treasure'.[165]

Two years after her appearance with the Royal Shakespeare Company, in the winter of 1973-74 Peggy once again appeared in a musical version of *Alice in Wonderland*, this time co-starring the singer Marianne Faithfull and ballet dancer Sir Anton Dolin. The play would reunite Peggy with Duncan C. Weldon, who in retrospect regarded Peggy as 'an important part of his career – especially at the beginning'.[166] She would also feature as the villainous Queen of Spades in *Queen of Hearts*, a television adaptation with Danny La Rue (as the Queen), which was screened on ATV on Christmas Day 1973. In between her frequent stage appearances during the mid 1970s Peggy also appeared on radio, notably as a panellist on the all-woman panel show *Petticoat Line*, and as a guest on *Sounds Familiar*.

The mid-seventies in many ways mirrored Peggy's career almost thirty years earlier as she appeared in an array of stage plays. In 1973 she was on home turf at the Palace, Westcliff, in Colin Morris's play *Jack and Knaves*; but the production received mixed reviews with one critic labelling it 'a shabby, artless piece without any merit whatsoever' and stating: 'The cast try bravely with their cliché characters but have no success. Peggy Mount resorts to her famous basso-profundo to struggle for laughs... but the author cannot develop the scene and the whole thing falls utterly flat.'[167] In the following year she featured in the Chichester Festival, playing 'the eternal mother' Mrs Amlet in *The Confederacy* by Vanbrugh (a star-studded production featuring a large number of star names including Dora Bryan, Frank Middlemass, Peter Gilmore, Gemma Craven, Nicholas Clay and Patsy Byrne); and in the summer of 1975 she spent three weeks as the central character of the mother in *The Anniversary* at the Everyman Theatre in Cheltenham, produced by Malcolm Farquhar. She later admitted that the role challenged her, something she conceded was a good thing but not necessarily something she could cope with regularly. Once again she was regarded as the best thing in it with one critic writing: 'The management is fortunate in having Peggy Mount, that greatly experienced actress of stage and television, to play the star part. She revels in the character and her possessiveness and domination are intermixed in such a way that the audience warms to her alone.'[168]

Amid the busy days of touring Peggy also made the news for a less than agreeable reason. In January 1975 her Leigh-on-Sea bungalow was broken into by Gordon James Best, 'of no fixed abode'. Luckily Peggy was away at the time and Best was reportedly caught by the police, under her bed, clutching a handful of her jewellery. He was subsequently jailed for eight years after admitting burglary and theft.[169]

A rare professional failure came for Peggy in 1976 when she starred in *Il Campiello* which was chosen for the royal opening of the National Theatre. Written in 1756, the comedy centres on the everyday lives of a group of people living in and around the Campiello, 'supposedly a thickly populated and very much alive square'. The production saw Peggy cast alongside fellow veteran Beryl Reid as a pair of widows. Remembered simply as

'The Italian play' by many of Peggy's friends and colleagues, it was directed by Bill Bryden who would later remember that Peggy was 'especially vivid' alongside 'the unique Beryl Reid'.[170] Despite decent previews it was slated by the critics:

> The wit is spare… The production has little atmosphere… The acting appears forced and superficial. Beryl Reid and Peggy Mount, as the widows, have one big scene together, when they chat and criticise while doing a domestic chore – in the middle of the square which has mysteriously emptied of all other life. They do their utmost to make the characters come to life and mean something, but unfortunately remain Miss Reid and Miss Mount.[171]

Bill adored working with both Peggy and Beryl and remembered the pair got on very well together. The failure of the production, he felt, was because it 'was like a little string quartet in a circus ring – too slight a piece for the panoply around it'.[172] Ian Talbot remembered it quite simply as a 'disaster'.[173]

Peggy received better reviews for her appearance as Mrs Jordan in the one-off television comedy *Just Like Mum*, screened in August 1976. Produced and directed by Stuart Allen and written by the prolific *Coronation Street* writer John Stevenson, the *Comedy Showcase* production also featured Mike Grady, Leonard Preston, Roderick Smith and Mark Rogers. It brought Peggy high praise:

> For what makes this show a potential winner is the presence of Peggy Mount… It is, of course, a character she has been playing for many years (slightly upper class from Mrs Larkins and Emma Hornett) but how superbly she does it… The voice – that rare amalgam of foghorn, rogue elephant and company sergeant-major – is as stentorian and flexible as ever. Her timing is impeccable… a performance full of zest and colour.[174]

Mike Grady, who went on to achieve fame in television series such as *Citizen Smith* and *Last of the Sumer Wine* (as Barry), would recall being 'a little in awe' of Peggy although he would also remember her as 'a very kind and thoughtful person who sometimes brought soup she had made for the company to rehearsals'. Despite spending just two separate weeks working together he was able to sum up very accurately Peggy's character: 'She was very professional, quite canny about people's personalities and also quite private.'[175]

Alas the idea was not picked up for a series and Peggy had to wait a further two years for another small-screen hit. Guest appearances on television in between her numerous perform-ances in the theatre in the 1970s did at least keep her in the general public's consciousness. In 1976 she performed a rarely heard music-hall favourite on television in *The Good Old Days* singing 'The World's Alright – It's the People Living In It', and in the same year gave a rousing performance in the period television play *Spice Island, Farewell!* by Terence Wheeler (and co-starring Peter Vaughan, Martin Shaw and June Page). While she did appear on several game shows at the time (and into the 1980s), she steadfastly shied away from the chat-show circuit favoured by many of her colleagues. In the meantime work in the theatre continued to keep her busy.

Teaming the notoriously acidic Kenneth Williams with any leading lady was always a tricky process for casting agents, especially in the theatre. In 1976 Williams was offered the leading role in the play *Signed and Sealed*, adapted from Feydeau by Christopher Hampton. A comedy based around accidental bigamy, it saw Williams cast as a middle-aged bachelor who is 'supposed to marry a well-off heiress but, owing to a registrar's mix-up, finds himself hitched to her fat, moustached mother instead'. With both Hattie Jacques and Joan Sims turning down the key matriarchal role, perhaps fully aware of how 'impossible' Williams could become during a long-running play, the role was finally offered to Peggy.[176]

Amazingly Peggy and Kenneth Williams managed to get on well during their time together on stage. Williams was notoriously unpredictable, especially towards his female co-stars, and over the years had developed a reputation for being 'difficult' to work with. His published diaries revealed his true feelings for many leading ladies. Fenella Fielding was labelled 'madam' and even Joan Sims, to whom he was a close friend, was considered 'so fucking suburban'. Age and longevity in the business were by no means protectors from his scathing comments and even veteran actress and former vaudeville star Renée Houston did not escape his wrath, albeit in his private diaries.[177] Peggy was luckier than most but perhaps was simply too strong a character for even Kenneth Williams to take on. Famous within the business for never suffering fools and for her utmost professionalism, it is difficult to see how Peggy could have offended her co-star in any particular way and as a result she escaped his criticisms during their time together.

Also among the cast of *Signed and Sealed* was a young Floella Benjamin, who would go on to become a familiar face on television in the 1980s before becoming a politician. She was one of many young actors whose lives were touched by Peggy's professionalism and in 2018, over forty years after their time together on stage, she would pay tribute to her colleague:

It was a great honour to work with the legendary Peggy Mount back in 1976 as I had grown up watching her on television. She was a very generous performer to work with and I learnt so much from her during that production. She had an unmistakable voice with the power to hit the back of any auditorium. She spent time working on her character to get it just perfect. She could see the funny side of any situation and shared that joy with those around her. Peggy was an inspiration to other actors both young and old. She was truly unique and gave joy and pleasure to all those who watched her performances.[178]

Opening at the Comedy Theatre in the famously hot summer of 1976, *Signed and Sealed*, despite its strong cast (which included Bryan Pringle, Paul Hardwick, Barry Stanton and Jane Carr), was a flop.

By 1977, the year in which Queen Elizabeth II celebrated her Silver Jubilee amid much pomp and national celebration, it had been over twenty years since Peggy achieved national fame as Emma Hornett in *Sailor, Beware!* Despite a string of successes on stage and television in the intervening years, in the Jubilee year Peggy managed once again to achieve critical acclaim in the title role of Brecht's *Mother Courage* at the Birmingham Rep. It was a powerful performance, still well remembered by her peers to this day, and probably her greatest professional success on stage since *Sailor, Beware!*

Peggy freely admitted that she had had 'no hesitation' in repeatedly turning down the role over a twenty-year period because of a fear she could not live up to the part, and also because she did not understand it. The persuasiveness of director Peter Farago saw Peggy change her mind, and she would concede: 'He's leading me by the hand and he's not undermining my confidence.'[179] Previously the part had been taken on by such powerful actresses as Dame Flora Robson, Miriam Karlin and Freda Jackson, each bringing different facets to the role, although Peggy had the advantage of having never seen the play and therefore was able to make it her own. She was fulsome in her praise of Farago, saying: 'This young man is the most exciting director I have come across for a very long time. I shall be surprised if he does not go to the very top of our profession.'[180]

The role was 'demanding' and Peggy found the play both mentally and physically challenging. It was a 'long' part, with masses of dialogue to learn, and she had to guarantee she knew the lines 'like the Lord's Prayer' to ensure the character (and the play) did not suffer. In addition, part of her role included clambering into a specially built wagon, and although she considered it to be 'the most wonderful stage prop I've ever been associated with' she also admitted this was not an especially easy task.[181]

Peggy's performance became iconic and the production was even filmed for BBC Television. While remembered by those in the profession and hailed by critics as one of Peggy's greatest triumphs, the play did not have the same impact on her career as *Sailor, Beware!* Having been a leading actress for over twenty years, it seemed that Peggy had now reached the pinnacle of her career and, no matter how great her performance, the tremendous boost she had received in 1956 could never be repeated. The Olympian heights to which she had risen following her time at the Strand Theatre had indeed been a once-in-a-lifetime occurrence.

The role brought with it excellent reviews. *The Guardian* regarded Peggy's characterisation as 'not merely a survivor...

but an unseeing dupe of the greed and corruption of the political system', whilst *The Daily Telegraph* wrote: 'She moved an audience without resorting to sentimentality… Her acting admitted no trace of self-pity or of the laughter she had been accustomed to provoke.' For the actress herself it was 'a dream part… involving comedy, drama, love and hate… I adored it.' [182]

In 1978 she starred in Ben Travers' farce, *Plunder*, at the National Theatre's Lyttelton, taking over the role of Mrs Hewlett. The cast included John Standing, Polly Adams, Trevor Ray, Basil Henson and Penelope Wilton who, despite their thirty-year age gap and limited time together, would remember Peggy to the author almost forty years later:

> I enjoyed working with Peggy very much. She was completely open and easy but I'm afraid I don't have any great insights. She was a lot older than most of us, so we didn't really move in the same circles. [183]

Both Peggy and John Standing received good reviews for their role in the production with *The Stage* writing: 'These two players are a joy; in their achievement and in the unobtrusive skill used to effect it.' [184] Once again it was Peggy who dominated the play:

> From her first cavernous 'Well?' upon her entrance, Miss Mount doesn't put a well-planted foot wrong. She gets the maximum effect from remarks like 'Me marriage-lines is in me ottoman', whilst her stiff, padded appearance enhances the unbudging manner in which she deceives all – without a trace of conscience. [185]

Plunder was also the start of a long and happy friendship with John Standing. Although John was aware that in many respects Peggy was a 'very, very private person', he also found her to be 'adorable – an exceptionally nice person – the nicest person you could wish to meet. She was a joy to be with.' Professionally speaking John also found Peggy to be the most agreeable of co-stars since she was 'very bright, extremely intelligent… always on top of it, on top of her lines and things like that'. He would also remember her agelessness and being 'surprised at how old she was when she died'.[186]

When Peggy returned 'home' to star in *Blithe Spirit* at the Palace Theatre, Westcliff, in the spring of 1978 it gave journalist Roger Diss a chance to interview one of the area's most famous daughters.[187] His resulting article, titled 'Peggy's Far From Blithe About Her Private Life' and published in *The Evening Echo*, gave a rare insight into the person behind the actress and his article made it clear that Peggy was equally as formidable as some of the characters she had played. This was not a lady to be trifled with.

Diss would describe Peggy as totally different from her on-screen persona and labelled her 'an enigma'. The article went on to say how Peggy would leave the stage door to be greeted by a small handful of loyal fans, not a large group of family and friends as would ordinarily be expected in a star's home town, and that she would return alone to her bungalow in Leigh. Likewise the article intimated that Peggy had all but forgotten her show-business roots, or indeed any of her roots, stating:

> Few of the friends she made during her amateur acting days in Leigh see her now. Her contact with local people is almost limited to a cheery greeting between her and shopkeepers on Leigh Broadway when she calls, but that is all. It is almost as if the star has come back to a vacuum.

Diss must have found Peggy a difficult interviewee. She 'refused' to discuss her private life, 'rumoured family differences' and 'parting of the way with old-time friends'. His questions were met with 'that frosty stare' famously used on stage and screen to generate laughs. In reality he felt 'the effect is withering – and silencing' as Peggy remained a 'closed book' when it came to her personal life. Peggy's ability to freeze an audience with a look was a talent she had also perfected in real life; '*That* look was very daunting' admits Eira Griffiths when remembering her old friend's sometimes icy glare.[188]

The only redeeming element of the encounter was when it came to discussing Peggy's work, which she was more than happy to do. When it came to anything even verging on personal details, Diss wrote that she radiated an 'aura of aloof secrecy'.

I keep myself to myself. Just because I'm known to the public through my work is no reason to air my private life in front of everybody.

Despite never forgetting her roots and maintaining a home in Leigh-on-Sea for decades, Peggy did not become a local 'celebrity'. She loved being in her home town where she lived a simple, private life, once saying, 'I'm quite happy being Peggy of Southend. The sea air is marvellous and I've got a lovely garden. My hobbies are tending my vegetables and listening to my LPs.'[189] Her circle of friends remained as selective in Leigh as it did in London. Few were permitted into her private world and she remained as discerning as ever in her choice of chums.

Leigh-on-Sea residents Cliff and Grace Stritten got to know Peggy well over the course of two decades via their neighbour Kathy Rastell who was one of Peggy's oldest friends. Cliff would recall how Peggy would ring Kathy 'out of the blue' and say, 'Are you free? I'm coming down.' Cliff recalls: 'While she was out shopping, people would sometimes say, "It is Peggy Mount, isn't it?" She'd just say "No".'[190]

Peggy was not averse to asking Cliff to mend household items and once travelled on the Greenline bus from London to Southend carrying a broken Hoover vacuum cleaner for him to repair. She also once returned to London on the bus clutching two bags of rotting horse manure she had been given on one of her 'country visits' for her garden.

Although an extremely private person, once established as a star of the theatre Peggy was always quick to lend her support to charity events and as a result was frequently called upon to appear in benefit functions and to attend charity events such as opening village fetes and festivals. Over the years these would range from opening the Theatrical Garden Party in Bromley in 1956 to being a special guest at the Silver Jubilee celebrations at King James I school in Bishop Auckland in 1977. Variety Club often called upon her support and she was also thrilled to meet members of the Royal Family at such events, notably being photographed with the Queen at Variety Club's 'Fall in the Stars' event in 1971, also attended by the Duke of Edinburgh and Princess Anne. Throughout the 1980s and 1990s Peggy continued to 'do her bit' when it came to supporting good causes. She often featured in events organised by or involving friends such as Park Follies and the annual Music Hall Gala, both at the Open Air Theatre, Regent's Park (1982 and 1985 respectively), and as late as 1998 was still attending charitable events.

Throughout the 1970s Peggy was very much a jobbing actress, particularly on stage. She happily admitted that the theatre was her 'first love' and that she was far more interested in the part and the playing of them than the money. While television work was undoubtedly more rewarding from a purely financial point of view, work in the theatre provided Peggy with the professional stimulation she craved.

6
Theatre legend

'She really was her own worst enemy'

A DECADE AFTER starring in *George and the Dragon* and following a long list of successful stage appearances, Peggy's role as Flora Petty in thirty-one episodes of *You're Only Young Twice* for Yorkshire Television brought her another major success on the small screen.

The series was set in Paradise Lodge, a large detached house for 'retired gentlefolk' and centred upon the antics of four of its residents, played by Peggy, Pat Coombs, Lally Bowers and Diana King. Written by Michael Ashton and Pam Valentine, *You're Only Young Twice* ran for four series and also included two Christmas specials. It was very much a vehicle for Peggy who dominated the series as the undoubted star. Impatient, intolerant and domineering, the character of Flora Petty was another battleaxe role for which Peggy was ideally suited.

During their years together on the series, writer Pam Valentine got to know Peggy well and provided a clear and objective view on the character of her famous colleague. On their first meeting Pam remembers initially thinking that Peggy was 'a bit fearsome', but was also conscious of her insecurities and realised very quickly that Peggy was 'pretty desperate for the work... for *something* to happen. She felt she was very much in the doldrums and she actually said at one point when we were making the pilot, "If this doesn't work I will cut my throat," which shook me because it showed how much she thought her career was on the slide.' Although the series was written very much with Peggy in mind for the lead character, Pam admits: 'I didn't realise at the time how very good an actress she was – Peggy could run the gamut. She could be very funny and then swiftly very touching.'[191]

Peggy herself admitted that for the previous five years television work had been 'lean' with appearances being 'few and far between'. It was true that most of her time during those years had been taken up with work in the theatre, but, ever practical, she also observed: 'Working in the theatre doesn't do any more than pay the rent.'[192]

Happily the success of the pilot resulted in the series being commissioned and even bought by overseas television companies. A steady amount of work and recognition for Peggy and her co-stars would follow. The 'lovely' cast, on the whole, worked very well together, without any of the bitchiness that may have been anticipated by bringing together a mainly female group of actors. Peggy herself was especially pleased to be working alongside Lally Bowers, whose professional career began in 1944 and included numerous successful plays in

London's West End. Like Peggy, Lally Bowers had toured the country in her early days in rep and was receiving praise from the critics at the very start of her career. Pam Valentine remembers that Peggy considered her fellow actress to be 'a genius – a superb actress' and constantly pushed for her to be given more lines, saying: 'I revere that woman – give her more, give her more.'

By now Peggy's friendship with Pat Coombs was well established. Their time together on the series perhaps cemented the relationship, which continued until Peggy's death. Like most people who ever encountered Pat Coombs, Pam Valentine remembers her as 'one of the loveliest people in the world', but was also conscious that the relationship between Mount and Coombs was 'a friendship that was organised by Peggy... She liked Patty very much to herself. When making the series she'd say, we'll sit here Patty, or we'll do that Patty; and Patty was so sweet.'

The relationship between the two ladies was also remembered by Georgina Moon who played Miss Finch in all four series of the programme. The familiarity between the pair meant that Peggy was more than comfortable in her on-screen physicality with Coombs, as Georgina Moon would recall to the author:

> Pat used to brace herself on the scenes they had together... Sometimes with the slapstick Peggy was very full-on, and if she had to slightly push Pat or give her a pat on the back, Pat was likely to go flat on her face! They sometimes had rather boisterous scenes together and Peggy would go a bit too far in rehearsals.

John Standing was well aware that 'Peggy was always playing gorgons and famous for her mental brutality – rather than her physical brutality – and her vocal brutality, her booming voice and all of that, but she was a darling.' It is fair to say that Peggy's physical strength, however, far surpassed Patty's. Yet, as with many aspects of Peggy's character, it is something Coombs managed to take in her stride.

The slapstick element of the series did not deter Peggy in the least. Despite being in her sixties and heavily overweight during the production of the sitcom, Peggy remained surprisingly agile and, like many larger ladies, incredibly light on her feet. Every element of the series was approached with complete professionalism and, according to Pam Valentine, 'There was no messing around.' The stark comparison between the tall, stick-thin, lanky frame of Pat Coombs and the short, stout figure of Peggy Mount inevitably led to the characters being likened to a modern-day female version of Laurel and Hardy. Aside from their physical differences, which were successfully incorporated into the humour of the series, many facets of the actresses' real-life personalities featured in the scripts; Mount as the blustering, dominant star of the sitcom and Coombs as her timid, easy-going sidekick often (but not always) reflected their off-screen friendship. As the years passed and Peggy and Pat Coombs grew closer, it was often Patty who turned a blind eye to the less engaging elements of Peggy's character. Despite their differences Pat remained loyal to Peggy and never more so than during the last several years of their lives.

Although very much the star of the series, Peggy remained, in the words of Pam Valentine, a 'very, very generous artist; she had no objection whatsoever to fellow artists getting the laughs. She would suggest things – that will be funny, do that –

but if she took against someone, that was it. They were out. She was ruthless and she would say if she didn't want them in the series again.' While Peggy was 'delightful with the other actresses', Valentine admits that veteran Irish actress Peggy Ledger was a prime example of someone who did not escape Mount's wrath. Ironically Ledger (born in 1900) was the only actress genuinely old enough to be playing a character in a retirement home, but her inability to remember her lines and occasionally 'fluffing one or two' frustrated the star of the show who was 'one hundred per cent professional and knew the lines; she worked and worked and worked and she never complained about lines being cut'. As a result of what Peggy Mount considered Peggy Ledger's unprofessionalism she 'quickly didn't like her'. Mount would stipulate to the writers that Peggy Ledger should have no more than 'five lines per episode' before eventually demanding that Ledger be dropped from the series, saying, 'That's it. I don't want her in it any more.' As Pam Valentine remembers, 'There was no messing about with Peggy Mount and as a result poor old Peggy Ledger got the push.'[193]

Another rift would have a larger impact on the series and its cast and crew. In 2017 Pam Valentine revealed that 'Unfortunately, for no good reason Peggy took against Michael [Ashton]. She wasn't rude but she ignored him – regardless of the fact that our combined work was keeping her way up there.' It was Pat Coombs who revealed to Pam Valentine that Peggy's dislike of Ashton stemmed from her belief that he was responsible for one of her actor friends being sacked from a theatre company. Pam Valentine remembers the situation with sadness: 'Mike was a very good theatre director and there was an actor in the company who simply wasn't very good and Mike in fact had to sack him. If Michael had been horrible to this man, who she had taken to her bosom, then she decided she wasn't going to like Michael. It was typical Peggy. She was very childish. She was very, very difficult.' Such was Peggy's dislike for the series' co-writer that she even threatened to boycott Pat Coombs's 1978 *This Is Your Life* tribute if Michael Ashton attended, warning Graeme Muir: 'If they invite him I won't go.' As a result neither Ashton nor his co-writer attended the event which later caused Pat to question where Pam and Michael both were. Likewise Peggy always refused to have a group photograph of the cast and crew because she would not be seen alongside Ashton. Pam believes Peggy's animosity towards Michael had a major impact on the longevity of the series, and even Peggy's television career as a whole:

> Silly old sausage! We could have gone on longer if she didn't have this insane dislike of Michael who was the sweetest guy – everybody loved him. I think she built up such a dislike; and thought she would be doing so many more things, but of course she didn't. She didn't take against me, and quite wanted me to be her buddy, but I couldn't cosy up to her and be her buddy; I had to take a pleasant line of always being courteous and friendly, but not being girly-girly with her. If she hadn't taken against Michael I think the series would have run longer than it did.

Peggy was fundamentally a kind person but, throughout her life, struggled to display affection or accept personal praise or thanks in any real way. Professional recognition was always well received, but allowing her steely veneer to slip in private in order to accept affection or thanks was difficult for Peggy.

A prime example of this personal trait was recalled by Pam Valentine:

If anybody mentioned they couldn't get hold of something or they were looking for something, nothing was said but the following Sunday at the read-through she would turn up and stuff something in their hands. She heard me say one day, 'Why can't you get a little metal teapot for one person?' and the following Sunday she walked into rehearsal and said, 'Teapot,' and shoved it in my hands. I tried to say, 'Oh Peggy, that's so thoughtful,' but she just said, 'Oh, doesn't matter…' She was almost embarrassed by her own niceness. She really was her own worst enemy. Her instincts were kind, but something in her prevented her from letting her guard down; obviously she'd had a weird childhood, and the difficult relationship with her sister. She never talked about her family at all. She had a very kind, poor, sad, lovely side to her.[194]

One of Peggy's colleagues on the series was Johnny Wade, whose fifty-year career in entertainment included singing in cabaret and work in films and television. He would play Roger the handyman in all four series of *You're Only Young Twice* and as a result got to know Peggy well. In 2017 he would remember her with frankness:

Peggy Mount was a very difficult person to understand; if she didn't like you, that was that! She was very generous on the one hand but quite vindictive and spiteful on the other. She would knit various items of clothing for members of the cast – none of which fitted – and poor old Patty Coombs had to model some at the rehearsal rooms through gritted teeth. She would also cook cold-water pastry pies which were inedible. Little gifts for the cast at the end of each series were another thoughtful gesture.

I would drive her up to Leeds for the show and she would let me use the car for the weekend and I would drive her home and pick her up the next day – except one day I forgot to pick her up for rehearsal. My God, did the shit hit the fan then; the whole cast waited for the explosion. Director Graeme Muir was having kittens and was mumbling 'Sorry' to everyone. She didn't disappoint when she arrived; she burst through the doors and kicked Patty's handbag the length of the room, glared at me and told Graeme she was not to be spoken to.

The other side to her nature became evident early on. For some reason she took against the writers, Pam and Michael (who created the series for her), and refused to talk to them and only took notes from the director, which was ludicrous, but this went on for the whole series. She refused to sit next to Graeme's wife at the cast meals, calling her 'that woman'. She was the star and everyone knew it. God help any of the extras who sat on her chair on set. The cast were great and very patient. Let's face it, we all needed the work; and it's recently been repeated on ITV4, so hopefully we should all be recompensed for our service.[195]

Peggy could indeed be a 'difficult' lady. Sir Ian McKellen, who worked with her at the beginning of his career, would remember one such occasion when the less attractive side of her personality was displayed:

Peggy was outgoing and friendly, though of course we young actors at Ipswich treated her with the utmost respect. After one matinee, she challenged me to a game of Scrabble in her dressing room. To this day I am sorry that I beat her because she was not used to it and that was the only time I saw her in the slightest bit grumpy.[196]

Peggy was never a good loser and disliked being wrong in any situation. Writer Pam Valentine confirms:

If something was said that she didn't agree with she used to go purple, scarlet in the face, and she used to sort of wattle like a turkey and she would say, 'I know I'm right. I tell you I know I'm right.' One of her favourite words was 'bizarre'. If there was anything she didn't understand she used to say, 'That's bizarre.'[197]

In the midst of mainstream television success came a one-off role as 'Opinionated Alice' in the television play *Stargazy on Zummerdown*, with Roy Dotrice, screened for the first time in the spring of 1978. Based upon 'a strange vision of what

Britain could be like in the 23rd century', it was one of Peggy's more avant-garde roles for which she was handsomely paid.

While *You're Only Young Twice* received some mixed reviews, it did manage to last for thirty-one episodes, running from 1977 until the summer of 1981. Peggy was by now in her mid sixties, well over retirement age for women at the time, but with no intentions of slowing down on her acting career. Sadly, in retrospect, *You're Only Young Twice* would be her final starring role on television. Over the next decade or more she would continue to make guest appearances, invariably with good billing, but they were token roles and she would never again dominate a series of her own. While Pat Coombs went on to achieve continued success on the small screen (notably in the children's series *Ragdolly Anna*, as Marge Green in *EastEnders* and latterly playing Prudence in *Noel's House Party*), Peggy on the other hand returned to her first love, the theatre, where work proved to be more challenging – both physically and mentally – but equally more satisfying to her as an actress.

In the immediate years following *You're Only Young Twice*, Peggy was once more performing regularly on stage. Scottish-born director Bill Bryden worked with Peggy again at the National Theatre in the winter of 1979 in a production of *Candleford*. The play was regarded as a National Theatre experiment which 'developed into gentle triumph'. Presented in promenade fashion, with the actors and audience moving around as scenes shifted, 'unexaggerated' performances were given by Valerie Whittington, Morag Hood and Mary Millar, with Peggy playing the gossipy postwoman.[198] In the autumn of 1980, shortly after returning from Hong Kong, where she worked for Derek Nimmo at the Hilton Playhouse in *Blithe Spirit*, Peggy starred in *Jubilee*, written by actor-turned-playwright Gawn Grainger, and co-starring Norman Eshley and Doreen Mantle. The play received mixed reviews, with one critic writing: 'A slightly subdued Peggy Mount characteristically shoulders the main burden – and what a weight it is.'[199] The play ran for just three weeks at the Yvonne Arnaud Theatre and plans for it to tour did not materialise.

Norman Eshley, fresh from three series of television's *George and Mildred* (in which he played Jeffrey Fourmile), would remember Peggy with affection in 2018 and recalled that the play was slightly 'weird', with Peggy and Doreen Mantle cast as two 'loony old ladies' who kidnap a young taxi driver (Eshley). Norman, who spent time on stage in his boxer shorts hand-cuffed to a chair, was deeply fond of Peggy and remembered her as endearingly 'wicked' and a scene-stealer. Lines that were guaranteed to get Norman a laugh would often be upstaged by Peggy deliberately dropping her walking stick or coughing. It was an old-school trick which ensured Peggy received the attention of the audience. She was, after all, the star of the play – and she knew it. Thankfully Peggy's wickedness did not perturb Norman in the least. The pair worked well together, despite a faux pas remembered by Norman: 'She said she loved my work but the best thing that I had done by a long way was Flashman in *Tom Brown's Schooldays*. I said, "Peggy, that was Richard Moran." Exit a very embarrassed Peggy.'[200] The most dramatic incident of the production occurred during rehearsals when Peggy was 'shot' in the eye by debris left behind in a (prop) pistol which had not been cleaned out properly. The accident resulted in Peggy being taken to hospital for treatment.

Peggy's character in the play was uncharacteristic: a timid, genteel old lady and seen as a total change in style. Norman remembers that she was keen to 'get away from the *Sailor, Beware!* image' but didn't have enough confidence in the play or its director for the change to really happen. She was back playing a more typical character in the following year when she starred in *Mrs Tucker's Pageant* as 'ferociously raucous' Mrs Biggs, co-starring with Jacqui Reddin, Judith Bruce, Larry Dann and Valerie Walsh at the Theatre Royal, Stratford East.[201]

Peggy's run on stage in *The Mating Game*, the national tour of which kept her busy in 1981 and 1982, brought her into contact with another iconic actress. Dame Barbara Windsor admits to being a 'fan' of Peggy's work and thought she was 'fantastic' during their brief time together. Although the two ladies didn't have much time to get to know each other well, Barbara would recall Peggy as 'a delightful lady and fun' and as someone who 'just got on with her job'.[202] Peggy's role as Mrs Finney was another formidable battleaxe-type character. Both she and Barbara Windsor nevertheless managed to stand out in Robin Hawdon's farce:

Highlights are Windsor's innovative striptease on the collapsible bed, contrasted with Mount's sudden appearance in a voluminous caftan surmounted by a large feather which conjures up a gargantuan Minnie Ha-Ha, all set to be wooed by her employer. It's foolish but it's fun.[203]

Another member of the cast was 1964 Miss World winner Ann Sidney (who in later years married Duncan C. Weldon). She would recall Peggy to the author via email in 2018:

She was fearsome to me! I was a little scared of her to be honest. She was okay with me but seemed abrupt – probably ambivalent regarding my background of being a beauty queen. Ha! She always had a chair at the side of the stage where she sat knitting in between her entrances. Always on cue and a complete professional. But I never really got to know her as she kept to herself on that tour. Perhaps I just wasn't experienced enough and she probably thought I was a flash in the pan. She may well have been right there.[204]

The 1980s saw Peggy return to pantomime and in this medium she would remain busy, almost annually, until the very end of her career. A number of her contemporaries avoided the slightly frivolous world of panto for various reasons. The whole genre was regarded by many as undignified and indeed viewed with an air of snobbery. Peggy's friend and former co-star Beryl Reid, upon hearing that Peggy was cast to appear as the Good Fairy in 1986, said, 'I should shoot myself if that happened to me at my time of life.'[205] It had been decades since Peggy's first appearance in *Humpty Dumpty*, yet her love of panto remained, despite the arduous physicality and elaborate and often heavy costumes involved in her parts (usually as Fairy Godmother of some description or another).

In 1981 she starred in *Aladdin* at the Pavilion Theatre, Bournemouth, alongside Roy Hudd, Clive Dunn (of *Dad's Army* fame) and the singer and actress Ayshea Brough, who was cast as Prince Charming. For Ayshea the experience of working with Peggy was an unforgettable joy as she recalled to the author in 2017:

We first met at rehearsals and I was really pleased to meet her because I'd watched her in so many television series and always found her hysterically funny and really great. I remember watching her during the rehearsals and she just had the script and was quite quiet and just read it through, and then they did a rehearsal and I remember that she lit up the stage – from the first day. She was just tremendous, and she had to be about seventy by then I think. She came out on the first night in full make-up and was just wonderful.

She was very, very sweet to me and talked to me a lot about acting. I told her that I wanted to do Shakespeare and she told me things that I could do. I just found her adorable. She just did her job, was never any trouble and just a nice woman. I really adored her. My fiancé at the time would take her car to wash it and she was so grateful. It was a nice thing I think for her – to have a man look after her.

I think she probably didn't suffer fools gladly but she was very, very loving towards me and I came in with great billing but just a little pop singer, but then she must have seen some other depth to me.

I was a mischievous little thing but she never said a word! I think if she could see you were dedicated to the job and you were a professional, that was all she wanted. In panto everyone always complains about the hours and the time and it's so exhausting – the actual pantomime – but she never complained: not a word.[206]

Despite living in the same hotel and sharing meals together during their time on stage, Ayshea and Peggy did not keep in touch, although as Ayshea admits, 'I would have seen a lot more of her but I moved to America and didn't come back until the year after she had died.'[207]

At Christmas time 1982 Peggy would again work with Ann Sidney, this time at the Theatre Royal in Bath, in the pantomime *Cinderella* where Peggy was also joined by fellow veterans Bill Owen and Jimmy Edwards. Further annual appearances would then carry on until Peggy was over eighty years old.

By the mid 1980s Peggy Mount was very much regarded as an icon of British entertainment; an actress who had proven her worth in every area of the profession. Yet even as she approached her seventies Peggy had no intentions of slowing down and her drive to continue acting resulted in her gaining work for the Royal Shakespeare Company where she received

An early publicity photograph of Peggy inscribed 'Don't be to (sic) scared Norman. I'm not so bad as I'm painted'

Peggy in the mid 1950s

A star is born. A glamorous-looking Peggy photographed by Eric Gray
following her dramatic rise to fame on stage in *Sailor, Beware!*

STRAND THEATRE

LONDON

Proprietors	-	-	-	**SEND MANOR TRUST LTD.**
President -	-	-	-	- **LIONEL L. FALCK**
Licensee and Managing Director		-		**R. L. WELLS, F.C.A.**

MONDAY TO FRIDAY EVENINGS AT 7.30
MATINEE: THURSDAY 2.30   SATURDAYS AT 5.15 & 8.30

BY ARRANGEMENT WITH SEND MANOR TRUST LTD

JACK WALLER

for Stories and Plays Ltd.

presents

A COMEDY BY

PHILIP KING and FALKLAND CARY

PROGRAMME

First Performance at this Theatre Wednesday, February 16th, 1955

The programme for *Sailor, Beware!* The play catapulted Peggy to stardom.

Relaxing on the set of *The Naked Truth*: Peggy and her co-star Terry-Thomas
(Photo: REX/Shutterstock)

Peggy (as Ada Larkins) and Shaun O'Riordan in the 1960 film *Inn For Trouble*

Peggy as Mrs Bragg in the 1966 film *Finders Keepers*

'I managed to spill gazpacho all down her white stole.'
Peggy (as the Nurse) with a young (Dame) Judi Dench in Zeffirelli's production
of *Romeo and Juliet* (Photo: ANL/REX/Shutterstock)

Peggy photographed in the 1960s
(John Alexander Studio,
Leigh-on-Sea)

Peggy Mount with David Kossoff, her co-star in *The Larkins*. The popular television series made her a household name.

The cast of *George and the Dragon*: John Le Mesurier, Keith Marsh, Peggy and Sid James (Photo: ITV/REX/Shutterstock)

Peggy on stage in Terence Frisby's *Bandwagon*, with Ron Pember and
Toni Palmer (Mermaid Theatre, 1969)

Well known for her love of driving, Peggy poses alongside her MG car in 1971
(Photo: ANL/REX/Shutterstock)

Peggy as Flora in *You're Only Young Twice* (Photo: Yorkshire Television)

Nancy Mount (Peggy's only sibling) photographed in old age. She continued to work until the night of her death in 2011.

Nancy, aged ninety-five, in 2007. The Mount sisters were estranged for half a century. (Photos courtesy of Philip & Sally Brazier)

A beaming Peggy photographed in the 1990s

Peggy with her beloved friend Eira Griffiths (far left)

Happy in a pinafore, Peggy photographed off-duty in
the 1980s. Away from acting she revelled in domesticity.
(Photos courtesy of Eira Griffiths-Darton)

'She was brave and brilliant.' Peggy, with Alec McCowen and Frances Barber, in *Uncle Vanya* (1996). It was her last major appearance in the theatre.
(Photo: Alastair Muir/REX/Shutterstock)

'Why do we look so glum?' Peggy, with Pat Coombs (right) and
Jean Fergusson (centre), in the autumn of 1999
(Photo courtesy of the late Pat Coombs)

'It was the perfect setting.' Peggy, with Eira Griffiths, at
Denville Hall (Photo courtesy of Eira Griffiths-Darton)

critical acclaim and some of the best reviews of her career. She would feature in a variety of plays for the company including *The Dillen*, *Measure for Measure*, *Mary After the Queen* and *The Happiest Days of Your Life*.

Peggy's time with the RSC was a success both professionally and personally and her sheer presence also made an impact on those around her. The company at that time featured a handful of young actors who went on to achieve notable success in the business, including Niamh Cusack, Tilda Swinton and Jane Horrocks. Niamh remembers Peggy as 'a stalwart, utterly professional and a good-humoured woman and in that she was influential to a young actress like me'.[208] Oliver Ford Davies, another colleague at that time, would remember thinking that 'Peggy was very pleased to be at the RSC doing serious classical theatre' and that she approved of him because 'I had craft and was audible – two vital things for her.'[209]

In 1984 Peggy starred in *The Happiest Days of Your Life* for the RSC. In her role as the principal of a private girls' school 'unwittingly foisted on to a boys' school shortly after World War II' she was labelled a 'marvel'.[210] The production was visited by the Prime Minister, Margaret Thatcher, who was photographed alongside Peggy – two formidable ladies, in two very different capacities, both flashing toothy grins for the camera. Working alongside Richard O'Callaghan, John Cater, Maria Aitken and Griffith Jones, her 'formidable principal-cum-dragon' brought cheerfulness to the production although the adaptation of John Dighton's farce received mixed reviews.

When the RSC's 1984 season in Newcastle was announced – with a total of sixty-four actors listed – Peggy was one of the star names, along with other well-known thespians including

Daniel Massey, John Thaw, Zoë Wanamaker, Gemma Jones, Richard Griffiths and Juliet Stevenson. During her time in the north-east, Peggy, by now deemed 'the Grand Old Lady of the stage', took time out of her commitments to accompany Juliet Stevenson to present awards to local schoolchildren who had won the annual Midland Bank poster competition.[211]

Peggy's time with the RSC allowed her, once again, to showcase her versatility as an actress, much to the pleasure of her friends, colleagues and fans. Georgina Moon was thrilled that her former colleague was able to continually spread her wings, especially in the theatre, admitting to the author: 'What was so lovely was she didn't just do comedy... she was able to do so much more.'[212] Peggy's role in *Measure for Measure* left one critic yearning for more and gushing: 'I am sure that Shakespeare, had he known Peggy Mount was to appear as Mistress Overdone, would have amplified that tiny part.'[213]

Penny Ryder co-starred with Peggy in both *The Dillen* (in which she played the 'indestructible' Cal Cook) and *Mary After the Queen*, where Peggy's main role was as an 'effective anchor point as Narrator'.[214] Penny adored her older colleague, remembering she was always the first person from whom she received a Christmas card every year until the very end of Peggy's life. Professionally speaking Penny considered Peggy to be 'marvellous' while also being aware of her slight 'vulnerability' in light of her advancing age. This vulnerability was a quality that was occasionally recognised by other colleagues in later years, and never more so than during Peggy's final stage appearance over a decade later.

One of Peggy's more lasting friendships gained from her time at the RSC was with the actor Ian Talbot. Having first worked together in *Mary After the Queen*, the pair would remain friends until Peggy's death. *Mary After the Queen* was based on a series of flashbacks in which Peggy's character described how she fell in love with a young man (played by Ian). He would later recall that he was 'one of the very few men to kiss Peggy Mount on stage'. The encounter delighted Peggy, as Ian remembered over thirty years later: 'She was hysterical when we had to kiss and said, "This is the moment I've been waiting for, Ian."' Another stage appearance saw the pair performing a tap-dance together which 'for some reason Peggy could never get right'. As the run went on this scene got bigger and bigger applause; little did Ian know that Peggy had given up on the routine and was making faces at him to the delight of the crowd. As Ian recalls, 'She was bringing the house down.'[215]

Ian adored Peggy and spent enough time with her to see various facets of her strong persona. He clearly remembers their time doing promenade theatre when she whacked an autograph hunter round the head and said, 'Do you mind? I'm acting.' Ian admits, 'I fell in love with her from then on… She didn't suffer fools gladly but she was a very kind person.' In her seventies and eighties Peggy remained one of Ian's stalwart supporters when he became Artistic Director of the Open Air Theatre in Regent's Park. Peggy's bluntness and fearlessness were seen by Ian when she later worked for him:

> I remember she pinned an actor against the wall who was complaining about working in the open air and said, 'Did you sign a contract?' and he said, 'Yes, yes,' and she said, 'Well, why the bleeding hell don't you shut up?' and she shook him against the wall. She was formidable.

On another occasion, at Broadcasting House, Peggy was enraged to be stopped by an over-zealous security guard after she had forgotten her identity pass. For once Peggy used her star status by retorting, 'I'm Peggy Mount!' Her face (and voice) not being proof enough, Peggy was still not allowed into the building and, as Ian remembers, 'She gave the security guard what for and there was a tremendous argument.'[216]

When Ian took over running the Open Air Theatre, Peggy would often appear in shows (notably performing limericks with Bernard Bresslaw) to help raise money for the theatre which was struggling at the time, rehearsing from two o'clock in the afternoon and then performing that same evening. Throughout their years as friends Ian found Peggy to be 'really warm and supportive' and he never failed to be impressed by her skills as an actress. He went on to direct Peggy in *The Good and Faithful Servant* – written by Joe Orton – and thought she was 'brilliant in it'. Summing up Peggy as a performer and as a person, Ian would admit: 'I liked her and thought she was extremely talented. My God she knew how to time a laugh. Her timing was spot on.'[217]

Another colleague struck by Peggy's intense professionalism was designer Claudia Mayer who worked with Peggy in 1987 in *Party Piece*, directed by Roger Clissold. While remembering Peggy as 'formidable', Claudia would also recall her as 'extremely professional – she was on point all the time – totally one hundred per cent. It was an honour to be working with her. A lesson.'[218]

The diversity of Peggy's career, especially in the 1980s, could not have been greater. While receiving critical acclaim for her work with the Royal Shakespeare Company, she also received popular acclaim for her continued work in pantomime. In the winter season of 1985/1986 she was 'uncontrollable' as a 'slightly unorthodox' Fairy Godmother in *Cinderella* at De Montfort Hall, Leicester, alongside Bill Maynard, Christopher Beeny and Patrick Mower.[219] The production was directed by Freddie 'Parrot Face' Davies who, at the age of eighty-one, would recount in conversation to the author how he considered Peggy a 'joy' to work with. He would also remember how Peggy served almost as an 'aunt' to the rest of the cast, happily sitting in the wings with her knitting watching the antics of her younger colleagues.[220]

Despite the physical rigours of panto Peggy remained as professional as ever into her seventies. A couple of years later in 1988 she was at the Palace Theatre Manchester – alongside Michael Barrymore and Bernard Bresslaw – where her role as the Fairy Godmother in *Cinderella* was regarded as both 'smashing' and 'nearly steals the show'.[221]

* * *

By now Peggy was living permanently in London: first at Montagu Mansions, two blocks west of Baker Street, and finally in a one-bedroom ground-floor flat in Devonia Road, Islington. The deaths of her last friends in Leigh-on-Sea eventually severed any remaining links with her home town and therefore made selling her bungalow a relatively easy task, but during the 1980s Peggy could still stay with friends in Leigh and would often visit other parts of the country while she was still able to drive. Her neighbours in London included actress Linda Robson (best known for her role in *Birds of a*

Feather); and here she was able to enjoy a small garden, in which she took great pride. In her heyday Peggy had famously kept a boat (aptly named 'The Dragon') and it was once reported that she ran it aground whilst out with friends, marooning them on the sandbank off Foulness when she misjudged the tide. With the boat now long gone and having never kept pets, although she 'always respected animal life', it was gardening which often occupied Peggy's spare time and her knowledge of plants and botany was not inconsiderable.

Her homes in both Leigh-on-Sea and London were remembered by Eira Griffiths as 'comfortable and welcoming – especially the sofas!' and over the years she accumulated a good selection of antique furniture.[222] While on tour round the country Peggy loved nothing more than driving herself around and visiting antique shops, picking up fine pieces of china or glassware in the process with which to decorate either one of her two homes. She remained happiest when entertaining friends, cooking, making jam or sitting quietly with her knitting.

Pam Valentine was an occasional visitor to Peggy's 'nice flat' and during their years together during *You're Only Young Twice* was invited for dinner. While many remember Peggy's prowess as a cook, especially when it came to traditional English food, Pam remains sceptical about the full extent of Peggy's culinary talents:

> She was convinced she was a very good cook. She talked about it a lot. She wasn't very far from Marks and Spencer – so when you had a meal with her it was 'Thank you Saint Michael' – disguised, but cooked by Marks and Sparks.[223]

Pam would also remember that Peggy was intensely proud of her culinary skills, even to the point of not allowing her on-screen character in *You're Only Young Twice* to be portrayed as a bad cook:

> We wrote an episode once where she cooked a meal and everybody got upset tummies because of it. It was a very funny script. The director, Graeme Muir, phoned me up and said, 'Oooh sweetie, sweetie, you're going to have to change the script.' I said, 'Which bit?' and he said, 'All of it!' Peggy had seen the script and said, 'I'm not doing this. I'm a very good cook.' So we had to rewrite it so that she was a very good cook and it was Patty who caused disaster by putting Epsom salts or something in the food and gave everyone the runs. When I saw it on the screen I thought, oh God.

Peggy's Christmas puddings were almost as legendary as the oversized knitted socks she produced as Christmas presents for close friends until the end of her life. Being honoured with one of Peggy's hand-knitted items was sometimes a mixed blessing. While Harry and Eira (Griffiths) Darton still treasure the items Peggy made, others have slightly different memories of some of her garments, as Pam Valentine recalled to the author:

> She very much liked Duncan Wood who was the head of light entertainment, a lovely guy. She wasn't silly about him but his word was law. She used to knit him things – she was a great knitter. Unfortunately the things she knitted would never fit. She once knitted him a waistcoat with wooden toggles on it. She complained that she hadn't seen him in it, so he had to put it on. It was perfectly obvious that one side of the waistcoat was longer than the other. She said, 'It's your toggles, you haven't got them right.' Peggy got hold of the shorter point of the waistcoat and yanked it down almost to his knees and said, 'There you are – it's perfect.' It wasn't – but she was happy! [224]

In her seventies Peggy remained very much a homemaker, delighting in entertaining friends and feeding colleagues, as Mark Curry would remember: 'Peggy cooked dinner for me at her home in London on several occasions and baked cakes which she would bring in to rehearsals. Good plain and hearty home cooking was her thing. She always asked me if I was eating well.'[225]

Life in central London suited Peggy in her old age. She was especially fond of visiting the theatre where she would frequently meet old colleagues and friends. Actress Patricia Franklin remembers seeing Peggy watching a performance at the National Theatre where she proved to be an enthusiastic member of the audience. While Peggy would never consider herself to be overbearing, she was not above inviting herself to stay with friends. Actress Damaris Hayman remembers: 'I used to occasionally bump into her because she was friends with a couple of young men who ran a bookshop close by in Cheltenham and she would stay with them for the weekend.'[226] The same friends, a gay Danish couple, were remembered by Pam Valentine who recalls: 'Peggy treated their house like a weekend cottage.'[227] When Peggy asked to stay, her friends rarely declined. Weekends in later years, and in particular Sundays, would often be spent with Harry and Eira (Griffiths) Darton and their children and grandchildren. Here Peggy was completely and happily absorbed into family life. Having worked together frequently on stage for years Eira saw both sides of Peggy's character and admits: 'We had a professional relationship and a family relationship.' It was with the Dartons in the last two decades of her life that Peggy found the security and comfort of family life, as Eira explained to the author:

> She loved home life; I think she felt she missed out on it with her own upbringing and upheavals with her sister and her own family. She was quite different with us than when she was with other stars...

Her humanity, her wanting to belong to a family, meant a great deal to her and I think she felt she belonged to our family.

It was an extraordinary relationship both professionally and family wise. We forgot she was a star. She knew that we weren't trying to get something from her other than friendship and humour.

I treasure what we had of her – which had nothing to do with her being a star, but she was that. If she walked into a room, she wasn't consciously trying to overpower everybody else but this was Peg... Peggy Mount. She was never a star when she was with us: she was just a human being, revelling in the antics of our grandchildren.

Although Eira admits that Peggy was 'not demonstrative', she was happy to 'sit and join in and was part of our family life'.[228]

In 1971 it was noted: 'In real life, Peggy Mount is not nearly as enormous as she appears on screen. She deliberately controls her weight – to keep the insurance people happy as well as for her own satisfaction – and she never goes above ten stone.'[229] Unlike her near contemporary Hattie Jacques – whose weight ballooned to over twenty stone by the 1970s, rendering her uninsurable for film work and beset by health problems – Peggy's weight never particularly impacted on her career or her health. Physically robust, she was rarely ill, remained light on her feet and surprisingly agile (as often demonstrated in *You're Only Young Twice*); and, despite some age-related health issues at the end of her life, she lived to the ripe old age of eighty-six. Like many of her generation, Peggy did smoke for a number of years, and in the 1950s and 1960s was often photographed with a cigarette in her hand – even in costume for *Romeo and Juliet*. Although she was certainly still smoking during the production of *George and the Dragon* in the late 1960s, it appears she managed to quit the habit shortly thereafter.

Peggy's weight nevertheless continued to increase in her sixties and seventies, not helped by her hearty appetite. According to Ian Talbot, Peggy's size was always 'a feature' but she was also seemingly oblivious to her food intake.

> I remember on one occasion she cooked two lasagnes and said, 'I don't understand it, Ian. I just don't understand it. I don't see why I put on weight.' She then divided one lasagne into four to be eaten by myself and three other actors and ate the other one on her own! I laughed so much and said, 'Peggy, could it be the amount you eat?' And she said, 'No! Rubbish! I hardly eat a thing.' She did laugh when I said, 'You do know you've eaten one on your own?' [230]

Peggy admitted again in 1977 the sentiments she had revealed over twenty years earlier: 'I was always very self-conscious about my size. I tried to slim when I was in my twenties but somebody gave me a good talking to and said that, no matter how I looked, I would always be a character actress. That made me cry my eyes out but I knew it was right. Ever since, it's been a lot easier to live with myself. It's done me a lot of good, too. I've always worked regularly – and I don't think that would have happened if I'd been beautiful.' [231]

Two years later Peggy's weight again featured in one of her rare interviews when she lamented: 'I have a thyroid deficiency – that's why I'm fat. There's nothing I'd like more than to lose weight. Obviously it has helped my career in many ways, but I'd still give anything to be slim.' [232] Designer Claudia Mayer, who worked with Peggy in 1987, remembers that although Peggy was 'co-operative in what she wore' on stage, she was also 'vulnerable' when it came to her size and in that respect had to be 'careful' with her costumes. Likewise her weight was 'not something to broach'. It also struck Claudia that Peggy had a yearning for 'romantic' roles but had long ago decided 'that was not for her'.[233]

Pam Valentine maintains that while Peggy 'could look lovely' she was 'not conscious about her size – she was too practical a person for that and understood her size was an asset. She was sensible enough to realise the battleaxe image helped make her money.'[234] Many people meeting Peggy for the first time were shocked that she was smaller than her on-screen image, while those closest to her were not at all conscious of her size. There were occasions throughout her life when Peggy did diet (Eira Griffiths confirms Peggy 'had this thing of dieting all the time') and in 1996 she would discuss, quite frankly, her lifelong battle with her weight. She reiterated that as a child she desperately wanted to be a dancer but, following her scalding accident and subsequent weight gain, realised she was too fat to ever follow such a career. Attempts to lose weight were inevitably short-lived and she revealed: 'I'd have an apple for lunch and a pear to go to bed with, hoping I would lose weight, and I would lose a stone but then I'd go back on to my normal diet and put it all back on in a month.' By the time of her last major interview, at the age of eighty-one, Peggy admitted that her lifelong unhappiness with her weight and appearance was no longer an issue, saying, 'I don't even think about it – but then I wouldn't at my age; why would I?'[235]

* * *

In the 1980s, as previously mentioned, Peggy toured for Derek Nimmo in the Far East, allowing her to see parts of the world hereto unknown to her, and she took great pleasure in performing the role of Madame Arcati in *Blithe Spirit* on several occasions. Although Margaret Rutherford appeared in the 1945 screen version, thereby immortalising the character in the public ethos, it was Peggy who very much made the role her own on stage. On one occasion she wore ankle socks as part of her costume which caused much amusement. They became a permanent fixture thereafter. One of her more high-profile appearances in the play was in 1989 at Nottingham's Theatre Royal, co-starring with Neil Stacey, Rula Lenska, Louise Jameson, Deborah Grant, Jenny Tomasin (much loved as Ruby in *Upstairs Downstairs*) and the ever loyal Eira Griffiths. Critics loved Peggy's performance. Terence Stevenson writing for *The Stage* thought the production was 'one of the best Coward productions I can ever recall'. Praise was also given to the star of the play: 'Peggy Mount, wrapped up in kaftans and string, was a manic Arcati, rolling her eyes and her r's with a fervid faith in her abilities to summon the dead.'[236] The company later toured the country with the production.

Peggy undoubtedly became a true seasoned professional in the role of Madame Arcati, a part she dearly loved and which 'followed her' for years. Louise Jameson, who regarded her co-star as 'brilliant', recalled the production almost thirty years later, revealing that Peggy's 'hearing had just started to go and she couldn't judge her own volume, *booming* in the wings, when she thought she was whispering!' A more poignant memory for Louise was connected to Peggy and her late mother, the amateur actress Marion Jameson:

As you know *Sailor, Beware!* was her *huge* success and in those days the amateurs were not allowed to perform anything that was being produced professionally, so when the rights to *Sailor, Beware!*

became available my mum's company (the Wanstead Players – or it may have been the Woodford Operatic and Amateur Dramatic Company) grabbed them. My mum got the coveted part and Peggy sent her a telegram (remember them?) wishing her good luck and saying she hoped she had a brilliant time with it. I still have it buried in the attic somewhere. My mum was so thrilled, really genuinely thrilled.

I opened *Blithe Spirit* on the anniversary of my mum's death, so it all became a rather complete circle, because even earlier in my mother's amateur career she too had played Elvira, one of her favourite parts ever. So, working with Peggy, the telegram, the memories of my mum talking fondly of Coward's amazing writing all slotted into place.[237]

Mark Piper worked with Peggy on a couple of occasions, including directing her in a production of *Blithe Spirit* at the Theatre Royal in Windsor. Despite having played the title role in the production on numerous occasions Peggy was still open to suggestions on how to tackle the role, as recounted by Mark:

I could have expected her to bring me a performance that she had previously honed to perfection. Not a bit of it: although she of course knew exactly how she had played it before and she could do it again. But she came with a completely open mind, was keen not to impose anything that was not wanted and made my life extremely easy. She probably, ultimately, gave her original brilliant performance but, throughout the rehearsal period, she had a great knack of making me feel that my contribution to her interpretation was great.[238]

Having enjoyed a successful run at Windsor, 'thanks to her', the production would subsequently go on tour with Lee Dean as the producer. During this time Peggy celebrated her birthday with a party organised by Lee. As Mark Piper would later remember, 'homage' was paid to Peggy by the entire company and she was showered with gifts 'which she opened with enthusiasm and gratitude, although because of her poor eyesight, she was probably not always sure what she was giving thanks for.' [239]

7
'Dame' Peggy

'I've had the most wonderful life'

ALTHOUGH SHE HAD KNOWN for years that she was often typecast, Peggy was a realist. While she openly admitted that playing romantic leads would have been a dream fulfilled, she also understood she was totally unsuitable for such parts. While grateful for the diversity of her work she knew her limitations, saying in 1971, 'A change of image? Rubbish. It's too late for that sort of thing.'[240] Actor and friend Mark Curry confirms:

> She had yearned to play romantic leading roles as a young actress but a certain director told her to abandon that desire as it would never happen and instead to embrace the fact that she could become a strong, memorable character actress. I reckon she managed this pretty well![241]

On the whole, Peggy's television appearances during the 1980s and beyond were relatively few; and to the public at large it probably appeared as if she were semi-retired. Yet they did in many ways display the versatility she had demonstrated on stage for years, albeit in a minor capacity. Despite approaching her seventies Peggy remained as busy as ever and during this decade delivered some of her finest performances, not least of course for the Royal Shakespeare Company. In the mid 1980s, television drama including *Punishment without Crime* (1985), *A Twist in the Tale* (1986, written by Ray Bradbury, in which she co-starred with Donald Pleasence) and a role in the all-star *The Trial of Klaus Barbie* (1987) also provided Peggy with the opportunity to show 'just what a fine actress she was'.[242]

Gareth Jones, who directed *The Trial of Klaus Barbie*, a courtroom-style drama so realistic it left many believing it to be a documentary, was especially pleased with Peggy's performance:

> She turned in a superb performance of finely controlled fury with very little rehearsal, the film being recorded in BBC Studio One even as the trial of that infamous genocide reached its climax in Lyon. When the Defence (Maître Vergès – David Calder) called up new and wholly unrelated witnesses, we twiddled our thumbs and eventually wrote them in. But Peggy, playing one of the torturer's victims, kept her nerve and her testimony passed, as I recall, in one single camera take, in what was an extremely compressed shoot. The film was finished and broadcast on BBC1 only four days after the final verdict.[243]

Peggy's ability to perform in dramatic roles was sadly rarely seen by wider audiences since most of her television appearances revolved around roles in situation comedies. Pam Valentine admits that although Peggy could be 'very, very difficult' she was also a '*very* good actress… She was very good, very touching, in bits of television in the 1980s.'[244] Unlike her near contemporary in age, Dame Thora Hird, Peggy was over-looked for such superb opportunities as Alan Bennett's *Talking Heads* series, for which she could have been ideally cast. Likewise she was never really given the opportunity to shine in a starring role in a serious dramatic production on television.

On radio in 1985 Peggy was cast opposite Liz Smith in David Scott's award-winning play *The Old Ladies at the Zoo*. In 2018 David would provide the author with a heartfelt tribute to Peggy, recalling her role in his work:

Peggy Mount played Bruno for me in my radio play, *The Old Ladies at the Zoo*. She and Liz Smith were the old ladies with co-stars Guy the Gorilla, the Flamingos, Sacred Baboons and various other inhabitants of London Zoo. Peggy played Bruno, a fighter to the end who was suffering from cancer and railing (quite rightly) against her fate. She was brilliant, totally unsentimental with a sardonic humour that fitted the part to a T. I hear voices in my head as regards characters but she was *beyond* any voice. We had a completely professional relationship; I don't think Peggy did 'personal' at work but I was aware of a great intelligence and very kind heart. The play won the *Radio Times* Drama Award – she was delighted on my behalf. Bruno identified in the play with Goldie the Eagle who escaped from the zoo and for some days eluded recapture – her delivery of the speech moved me and everyone else who was lucky enough to be in her audio presence. A trouper. a beautiful actress, a lovely human being.[245]

Interspersed with occasional serious appearances were more lighthearted productions. Peggy was not everyone's first choice for a role in *Doctor Who*, although given that many stalwart actresses were given guest appearances in the series throughout the 1980s (notably Sheila Hancock, Beryl Reid, Joan Sims, Brenda Bruce and Elizabeth Spriggs), it is perhaps not altogether surprising that she would also appear in the cult classic. Her two episodes as the Stallslady in *The Greatest Show in the Galaxy* saw Peggy make an impression on Sylvester McCoy, playing the Sixth Doctor in the iconic series, and over thirty years later he would remember thinking at the time, 'Wow, I'm working with Peggy Mount.'[246]

The children's television series *Trouble with T-Bag* showed that Peggy, at the age of seventy-five, had lost none of her presence or professionalism. Although Georgina Hale recalls that the production was simply 'too busy' to allow her to become well acquainted with Peggy, she would recall her co-star as 'a very large lady with this wonderful voice who arrived knowing all her lines from day one'.[247] A few years later she was 'crossing swords' with Frankie Howerd in his 1991 children's series *All Change* (in which she played Aunt Fanny). It was a case of inspired casting and introduced Peggy to a new generation of television viewers.

Throughout the 1980s Peggy continued to be extremely busy in the theatre. Indeed there were few actresses of her age who were so prolific. In 1986 she appeared again in *Rookery Nook* (directed by Mark Kingston), at the Shaftesbury Theatre, co-starring with Tom Courtenay, Ian Ogilvy, Lionel Jeffries and Nicola McAuliffe. Also among the cast was Christine Lohr (who in later years would play Mrs Bird in *Downton Abbey*) who understudied for the character of Gertrude Twine. Over thirty years after the production, Christine would recall to the author the occasion she was required to go on stage for three performances:

> There had been no rehearsals with the main cast and, with two hours to 'curtain up', I found myself quickly running through my scenes with the stars.

Peggy was very strict. There was a farce routine whereby she and I delivered quick-fire dialogue, whilst stepping up and down a flight of stairs. She wanted the timing to be exact and kept saying, 'No, you must be on the third step when you say that word and on the second step to complete the sentence. This is very important for the comedy timing to work!' I was in awe and petrified. However, it all worked out well.

Afterwards, a call came over the tannoy, that I should report to her dressing room. My heart sank. I felt sure I was going to be told off. I knocked on her door and prayed. She invited me in and was very complimentary. Phew!

She remarked that my role needed the strength I was able to bring to it. We had a little chat and, in passing, she mentioned she would never do commercials! 'They are not what one has been trained to do.'

I have always admired her unique presence and professionalism. A staunch lady with a very kind heart.[248]

Inevitably not all of Peggy's co-stars were drawn to her. Although generally speaking Peggy tended to respond better to men than woman even in her seventies, by which time she was quite rightly regarded as almost untouchable within the profession, Peggy could remain 'difficult' with co-stars of either gender. One leading actress would admit to the author, 'I do not have happy memories of my time working with her,' so much so that she was unable to share any recollections of Peggy 'that would do her credit'.[249] Another leading actor would recall Peggy bizarrely playing her lines directly to the audience one night, rather than to her co-stars, because some unknown matter had clearly upset her. It was, admittedly, a one-off occurrence but demonstrated that, despite her well-known professionalism, Peggy had the ability to be unpredictable.

On the other hand those of the younger generation were able to benefit from her experience, including Mark Curry who remembers:

> I performed in two plays with her: *Move Over Mrs Markham* (UK tour 1989/90) and *The Happiest Days of Your Life* (a production celebrating 1,500 plays at Windsor Theatre Royal in 1994). I also appeared in two theatre galas with her.
>
> Peggy gave me great advice on how to get good laughs and audience response. She told me that it was always best to get one huge laugh on a line rather than two small ones (something I've remembered ever since). She also insisted on clarity and volume with dialogue; 'It's no use if the audience can't hear you,' she would say to the younger actors in our plays.
>
> Peggy was, in my experience, a very kind, funny, warm-hearted person with a wonderful sense of humour and a roar of a laugh. She actually was basically quite shy and didn't open up to many people. She was a Taurean and, true to that sign, very earthy and homely. She loved good basic food, plants and nature and didn't like pretence of any kind. She was slightly impatient with some people. During the two comedy plays I did with her, she was very 'motherly' towards me, giving me advice and sort of looking after me.[250]

In the 1990s there came a handful of television guest roles, including an appearance in *Casualty*. In 1992 she played Mrs Weaver (the widow of the Great Shandoo) in *A Dream of Dracula*, an episode of *Virtual Murder*, a short-lived BBC Pebble Mill detective series. Donning a flaming red wig and flamboyantly coloured kaftan and jewellery, she was characteristically distinctive during her relatively brief appearance opposite Nicholas Clay (with whom she had previously worked on stage) and Kim Thomson, playing an investigative psychologist and his girlfriend. The series was created by Brian Degas and Harry Robertson, with three episodes being directed by

Philip Draycott who would remember the series to the author in 2017:

I thought of it as being like *The Avengers* – cheerful, fun, cast with lots of faces who were able to get on with it. Episode 5, written by an American, was about vampires and I cast names, which included Julian Clary and Peggy Mount and various others. Peggy only had one scene. It was all shot in and around Birmingham (where I'm from) and I was keen for the Roundhouse to be the location.

Peggy was obviously not in great health. She had trouble with the lines, but given that I was casting older established names often towards the end of their careers this was not unusual to be honest. I think Peggy just had the one scene in the Roundhouse in Birmingham... talking to the main characters, Nick Clay and Kim Thomson. It would have been two hours' work really.

She was a 'name' and I was casting the likes of Alfred Marks and Bernard Bresslaw and she fitted that mould really. We also cast Jon Pertwee in his last-ever screen job, so we certainly clocked up our pensioners.

She was a treat to work with – she was lovely. Of course I was a bit in awe of her having seen her in so many films. She was a bit doddery but was totally professional and a treat. She was very, very professional in that she turned up on time, did what was asked and left.

I remember her mostly from TV... *George and the Dragon*. She was always playing battleaxes, poor woman. She wasn't in the least like that when I met her. She was a charmer. She was a professional charmer, a professional actress. She was on time and did whatever was asked. She was a real character – a lot of those old-timers were!

I also recall she was annoyed and frustrated at not being able to remember all her lines – she was not used to that at all... Professional actors get very cross at themselves if they are struggling with the lines because they know they are holding everyone up. It must have been very difficult – a real struggle.

She obviously enjoyed doing the job and was very pleased with the engagement.[251]

Despite spending less than a minute on screen, Peggy was given decent billing for her guest appearance as a Sister of Mercy nun in *Fat Chance*, an episode of the popular television series *Inspector Morse*. Now larger than she had ever been in her life, Peggy's size was almost alarming; and, both physically and vocally, she dominated her brief scene alongside John Thaw.

This tiny appearance on the small screen should have catapulted Peggy to more prominent dramatic roles on television and even on stage. Her cold, almost demonic appearance opened up a new element to Peggy's characterisations and it was clear that at this stage in her career she would have been ideally suited to 'darker' characters. Sadly this facet of Peggy's acting ability was not explored. Perhaps this was through choice, since she had rarely worked in anything other than comedy on television, but also due to the constraints now placed upon her by the passage of time. Physically Peggy was now struggling with her mobility (although this was never demonstrated on screen), and it was also becoming harder and harder for her to learn the huge chunks of dialogue required for significant roles on television.

After an absence from film roles of more than twenty years Peggy's voice-over role as the Goblin Queen in the animated feature *The Princess and the Goblin* earned her a mention in Welsh cinema history. Directed by József Gémes, and released in Britain in 1992, the film featured the vocal talents of a range of star actors including Claire Bloom, Joss Ackland, Rik Mayall and Mollie Sugden, and was the first-ever animated feature film from Wales. Despite an impressive production budget, it bombed at the box office.

Like a number of other excellent actresses, Peggy certainly missed out on significant serious dramatic work on television in her old age as a result of typecasting. Her ability to portray both fragility and fierceness should have been capitalised upon in television roles. Peggy's sheer physical presence and, at times, steely blue-eyed gaze arguably could have been used to stunning effect in the hands of a forward-thinking director. Alas it was only on stage, mainly in her penultimate performance and even then in a relatively small role, that she was able to convey different facets of her acting repertoire to an audience. Of course such work, whilst seen and enjoyed at the time, does not live on in the way of film or television productions, and as a result Peggy's range as an actress is often forgotten.

Despite this it is worth noting that she undoubtedly acted as a pioneer in the profession. Unlike many of her contemporaries Peggy was able to tackle an array of roles, especially on stage, and thus prepared the way for the next generation of actresses (for example, the likes of Dame Julie Walters and Dawn French) who have gone on to enjoy amazingly diverse careers, despite starting out as comedy performers. The barriers of typecasting, although still problematic for many in the profession, are nowhere near as prominent as they were in Peggy's day. Undoubtedly her ability to perform as successfully in productions staged by the RSC as she did in children's television helped to break down some of those barriers.

* * *

Pantomime, that most 'British' of theatrical entertainments, has been the staple of many actors' careers for decades and a welcome annual source of income for some of the country's most popular actors, singers and performers. From 1988 Peggy would be kept busy with almost annual appearances in panto that would continue for the remainder of her career.

In the season of 1992/3 she returned home to Leigh-on-Sea to play a 'dotty' queen alongside *'Allo 'Allo!* star Richard Marner as king in *The Pied Piper of Hamelin*. The production starred Wayne Sleep, and also featured local disc jockey Peter Holmes who recalled Peggy to the author:

> She had these small but thick glasses (like the bottom of a Coke bottle only much smaller in diameter) which she took off to read her script at rehearsals. When she was on stage, we had to face her so she could see our faces to enable her to lip read… although she never appeared to be deaf, actually!
>
> She was quite stern sometimes in her character which enabled her to play the parts she played with such fearsome force, but she delivered her lines beautifully and had a natural knack of good timing and making people laugh. She was also very supportive and constructive in helping me to have a greater presence on stage.
>
> She lived in a largish bungalow on the corner of Elmsleigh Drive and Picketts Avenue in Leigh-on-Sea… She was quite a celeb locally… people would point out her home as they passed. Quite a character and very much her own woman! [252]

Many colleagues and fans thoroughly enjoyed Peggy's performances and were pleased to see her continuing to work. Jeffrey Holland remembers seeing Peggy at the Theatre Royal in Plymouth in 1990 in a performance of *Cinderella* ('while she could still see and walk'). He would recollect her performance of the Fairy Godmother as a breath of fresh air: 'It was nice to see her being a goody rather than a battleaxe.' [253]

Writing for *The Stage*, Neil Bonner admired Peggy in *Cinderella* at Crewe: 'Veteran Peggy Mount, as the Fairy Godmother, sportingly dances with Sleep in a comic routine, proving she can still make us laugh';[254] and as late as 1995 she remained sprightly in yet another performance of *Cinderella* at Redhill with one critic writing: 'Mount as Fairy Godmother made a splendid motherly good spirit. She went to the ball too and danced the Swan Lake cygnet divert with the master [Wayne Sleep]. Sleep described it as Swan Pond.'[255]

* * *

The 1990s brought Peggy into contact with numerous other actors and actresses: some new faces, and others, old colleagues. Poignantly she was reunited with Hazel Bainbridge (the mother of actresses Kate O'Mara and Belinda Carroll), with whom she had worked in rep decades earlier, in the stage play *A Touch of Mink*.[256]

During a charity show at the Crewe Theatre at the end of the decade Peggy was introduced to actress Jean Fergusson (best known for her role as Marina in over 200 episodes *of Last of the Summer Wine*) when they shared a dressing room. Jean was delighted to be in the presence of the veteran actress and over twenty years later would recall their brief encounter:

> I was thrilled to be in her company, having admired her for many years. It was quite bizarre though as I was dressed as Hylda Baker, and then Patrick Fyffe (aka Dame Hilda Bracket) joined us and I ended up helping them both get dressed! What a sight and how I wish I had a photo of the three of us.
>
> However, the main point of this is that Peggy was to introduce me on stage as she had a very funny Hylda Baker story to tell. She

said to me, 'I hope you don't mind but I have great trouble with names. I know you are Jean Fergusson but I'm worried I'll have a mental block, so as we are entering from the side of the stage would you mind saying your name over and over again just before I go to introduce you?' I didn't mind at all and when the time came there we were in the wings together; but just before she went on, the stage manager came to me and said my entrance had been changed and I was to go on from the other side and to get there quickly, so I had to leave her. She watched me disappear, looking somewhat concerned, and went on stage, told her story about Hylda, got a reaction, and then said, 'And now ladies and gentlemen I would like to introduce you to... (pause) Miss (another longer pause) ... Janet Frobisher!'

She apologised profusely afterwards but I really didn't mind. It made me laugh and many friends today call me by that name, in fact I recently got an email from a long-lost friend in Spain headed 'In search of Janet Frobisher'! [257]

A flamboyant cameo appearance in the children's sci-fi television series *The Tomorrow People* would be Peggy's final acting role on the small screen. Playing Mrs Butterworth, an actress hired by casting agent Quentin D'Arcy (played by Ian McNeice), Peggy performed the role with gusto at the age of seventy-nine. Determined as always, she projected no sign of age or frailty and vocally remained as strong as ever. Typically, she bellowed through two scenes and appeared sprightly and totally in control.

The episode was directed by Niall Leonard who would remember Peggy's 'consummate professionalism and amazing skills'. The role was filmed in one day under slightly difficult circumstances as Niall recalled:

The shooting scripts were timed, halfway through production, as running about 40% short. The writers, in a panic, padded the show out for all they were worth. They explored a thread where our heroes went looking for the casting agent of the goons who had played parts to mislead them in their investigation.

There was no money left for the scene – the budget had been calculated from the too-short script – but the producer grudgingly coughed up some extra cash, and the 'casting agent's office' set – in Acton, I think – was conjured up from nothing. Peggy was the centrepiece and carried all before her like a force of nature.

God, it's such a privilege to work with great artists when you're up against it on a tiny budget. And they never grumble or act the diva – actors like Peggy had known real hardship and penury and took tight budgets and lack of time in their stride.

I should add that her scene was with Naomie Harris, who went on to get an Oscar nomination for her stunning performance in *Moonlight*, and also plays the latest Miss Moneypenny to Daniel Craig's Bond. We'll be seeing lots of Naomie Harris in future, I suspect. I suppose that's the magic of acting – veterans passing the torch to stars of the future… if only by coincidence.

Despite the brevity of her appearance Peggy's performance was impeccable and remains remembered by the episode's director over twenty years later: 'She came to set, did her job brilliantly, and departed, leaving us the richer.'[258]

Although by her late seventies Peggy's work rate began to slow slightly, there were still appearances in the theatre to be had, notably with Patrick Cargill in *The Happiest Days of Your Life* at the Theatre Royal Windsor in 1994. It was another play whose cast included Eira Griffiths, who was now a constant and faithful figure at Peggy's side. Having already appeared in the production for the RSC, Peggy agreed to do the play again for Mark Piper; as he recalls, 'for Windsor money – not much!' Mark would reveal that Peggy's failing sight and mobility now made exits and entrances difficult for her, yet she loved doing the show and he would remember her 'spirit of cooperation, her sense of theatre and her pluck. That was Peggy.'[259]

Throughout her life, despite always being overweight, Peggy enjoyed good health and had a strong constitution. Physically she was tough and, until her eighties, often belied her age. John Standing remembers being 'surprised at how old she was when she died' having believed she was at least a decade younger than her actual age.[260] While her final television appearance saw Peggy striding purposefully in flat white shoes (wearing a flamboyant black cape and black-and-white feathered hat), by her late seventies she was inevitably beginning to suffer from various age-related ailments. By 1997 the indomitable actress had undergone two hip-replacement operations and also had a pacemaker fitted to treat an underlying heart condition.

* * *

By the time she reached her seventies many members of the public quite naturally assumed that Peggy had been formally recognised for her long and successful career; and, as a result, she was often addressed as 'Dame' Peggy, as Eira Griffiths would write: 'Her public for years always believed she was a Dame and often addressed her so. It amused her, but she always truly rated the honour they did her by mistakenly believing that she had already received this title.'[261] Like many of her ilk, Peggy was justifiably proud of her status as a star actress and worked hard to maintain it. She had seen a wave of leading ladies come and go over the years, especially in the late 1950s and early 1960s when beautiful actresses were propelled to Olympian heights by studio publicists and media hype, only to disappear into obscurity within the space of a few short years. Becoming a star of stage, screen and television was no mean feat, but sustaining a career in leading roles over a forty-year period was an incredible achievement, especially in light of Peggy's humble beginnings. Official recognition for Peggy came when she was over eighty years old. In the 1996 New Year's Honours List it was finally announced that Peggy Mount had been awarded the Most Excellent Order of the British Empire (OBE, civil division) for services to drama.

Peggy's investiture at Buckingham Palace on 12th March 1996 was her last major public appearance. Accompanied to the Palace by Harry and Eira (Griffiths) Darton, Peggy, just weeks away from her eighty-first birthday, was assisted by an equerry as she was presented to the Queen to receive her OBE insignia.

Outside the Palace after the ceremony Peggy was greeted by a large contingent of press photographers. Sans make-up, she was photographed wearing a large-brimmed black hat with a white trim. Holding her OBE insignia aloft for the cameras, Peggy was clearly beaming with delight. Her long overdue 'gong' was the culmination of a lifetime on stage, screen, television and radio, and it was especially poignant that it came as her career was drawing to a close. The girl from Southend, who became an overnight star in London's West End, had now come full circle. By now a beloved national treasure (although she would never say so), Peggy must have taken some satisfaction in her incredibly successful career and its – and her own – longevity. In the same year she would admit on radio, 'I've had the most wonderful life,' and those closest to her did not doubt it.[262]

Peggy's appearance in the all-star production of *Uncle Vanya* at the Chichester Festival Theatre was her most significant stage role of the 1990s, not only because of the calibre of the production and her own touching performance but also because it was to be her final major appearance in the theatre. The play saw Peggy reunited with director Bill Bryden, almost seventeen years after they had worked together at the National Theatre, and her friend Duncan C. Weldon. Following time at Chichester, the play later ran for two months at the Albery Theatre.[263]

The play received mixed reviews with Darren Dalglish describing it as 'a bit of a dull affair' and 'a bit depressing'. It was only the cast who managed to inject some enjoyment into the production:

> It is the acting of a great cast that saves the play from being totally like the story, 'boring'. The great Derek Jacobi (Uncle Vanya) is the star, of course; he can do no wrong whatever he acts in... We also have the delightful Peggy Mount who played Marina, the old nurse. She played the part to perfection and provided some nice comic touches. Without these and the rest of a great line-up of Trevor Eve, Frances Barber, Imogen Stubbs, Constance Cummings, John Normington and others, the play would have died.

Although Sir Derek Jacobi admits that he and Peggy didn't have much contact with each other either on stage or off stage since they both 'had their own circles', he was particularly pleased to be working with the veteran actress whom he remembers as 'a lovely lady... very gentle, very kind – quite the opposite to the Peggy Mount I expected to meet and quite unlike the big stentorian-voiced harridan that she often portrayed'. Jacobi's 'stark' memory of Peggy was her failing sight which he described as 'pretty bad'. The disability caused frequent mistakes on stage:

> Her sight was so bad... Her first entrance was coming on and pouring tea out of the samovar into cups for us all. And she used to put it on the floor and miss the cups entirely! Every time she did the scene she would be pouring tea all over the place.

Thankfully Peggy's role was adapted so that she had very little movement around the stage and spent most of her scenes sitting down, and (perhaps crucially for safety reasons) she was also sitting down when the curtain went up and when it came down.

As ever, Peggy delighted in her work and being in the company of fellow artists. As Sir Derek remembers:

> She was very trusting – there was nothing of the star about her – she was one of the company... I don't think she suffered fools very gladly, but she enjoyed the feeling of being in a company and being surrounded by a lot of younger people. I think that was sort of comforting to her. The role of Marina also allowed Peggy's vulnerability to show.
>
> The image most people had of her was from *Sailor, Beware!* She was totally different in *Uncle Vanya* – maybe to do with her age and her sight, but she was much frailer and much gentler – physically and vocally. There was none of that shouting... She was playing a character – it wasn't her.

Thankfully she received favourable reviews for what effectively turned out to be her swansong in the theatre:

> Peggy Mount as nursemaid Marina fulfils the role of everyone's confidante admirably – being approachable and predictable yet always kindly and patient, while maintaining an unusual relationship with the whole household in which she was a servant.[264]

Recalling their last professional engagement together, Bill Bryden would write: 'She was an original... Even when her eyesight was failing she was brave and brilliant in my production of Chekhov's *Uncle Vanya*.'[265]

In 1996 Peggy also returned to the Theatre Royal Windsor as one of many guest artists lending their support to a charity gala to aid the theatre which was facing temporary financial difficulties. At the end of the event Peggy had to thank Mark Piper, and in the process momentarily forgot his name. Although 'mortified' by the faux pas, Peggy and Mark later laughed about the mishap, leaving him with a lasting memory of Peggy's sense of fun.[266]

It is often said that Peggy lost her sight completely during her run in *Uncle Vanya*. This is not strictly true. However, it was at this time that her sight took a dramatic turn for the worse from which there would be no recovery. Following her triumphant role in the Chekhov production, there was yet another appearance in panto for the 1996/97 winter season when she played Fairy Kindheart in *Jack and the Beanstalk* at Poole's Towngate Theatre. It was a small role, again opposite Wayne Sleep, for which she received good reviews. Christopher Day, writing for *The Stage*, commented: 'Peggy Mount deserves funnier lines benefitting her professional stature, but shines in a brief Swan Pond partnership with Sleep.'[267] Renowned panto player Nigel Ellacott described to the author how he met Peggy at the end of her career and that she 'wasn't happy' as they sat chatting: 'She had by that time extreme difficulty with her vision, and I think the whole process of being on stage was unsettling as a result.'[268] Despite her near blindness Peggy managed to make her way through the production, but *Jack and the Beanstalk* proved to be her final appearance in the theatre. At the age of eighty-one Peggy's acting career had finally ended.

* * *

It was known to those close to Peggy that she had struggled with her vision for years. The problem stemmed from detached retinas and gradually became more serious and life-changing with age. Yet even in her fifties she was photographed wearing thick spectacles when reading scripts during rehearsals for *George and the Dragon*. During her 1996 *Desert Island Discs* interview Peggy would admit to the problem but emphasised, 'I can see on the stage; as long as I know where everything is I'm perfectly all right.' She also conceded that friends and colleagues were very 'helpful' and that her lines were now learned with the assistance of a cassette machine: 'A very dear friend puts it all on tape' (the dear friend was Harry Darton). After a lifetime of reading lines on a page Peggy found it difficult to adjust to this enforced way of learning, admitting that it was 'much easier to read the lines'.

Throughout the 1990s colleagues had noticed Peggy struggling with her vision, including Mark Curry:

Peggy's eyesight was failing slightly when we worked together which worried her but no one in the audience would ever have known. She would take extra time to walk around the set during technical rehearsals, thoroughly familiarising herself with doors and props etc. She had to have her script enlarged in order to learn lines and couldn't make notes, so she had to remember what the director wanted her to do. She arrived on the first day having learned all her lines. She was very strong physically, however, and had great stamina, plus of course that famous belting voice which was as powerful as ever. I cannot remember her ever fluffing a line. I worked with her really at the end of her career but she was still so excited and enthusiastic about our productions. Peggy would be sitting in the wings well before her first entrance. She felt it was so important to feel how it was going and what the audience reaction was like. She would concentrate and get herself in character – no idle chat or gossiping.[269]

Perhaps conscious of how her loss of vision could hamper future opportunities to work, Peggy played down the issue by saying, 'I can see: I'm not blind, I'm what they call half sighted,' and reiterated her desire to carry on working when she stated: 'I don't want ever to retire because I love working so much. As long as they want me I will be only too pleased to play.' For Peggy the thrill of a live audience was a drug she still craved. Indeed she admitted the 'buzz' received from working in the theatre, whether in serious roles or even panto, was like 'nothing in the world'.

Going blind – and at the end of her life Peggy was indeed registered as blind – was perhaps the most catastrophic event of Peggy's life and career. The positivity demonstrated in 1996 soon dwindled. She later admitted of her plight: 'The audience had no idea. But… I lost my nerve… my greatest regret. It was always my wish to die working.'[270] With her confidence shattered, Peggy regretfully but realistically realised that her acting days were over. By the end of the year her sight had deteriorated to such a point that she was forced to cancel her planned appearance in pantomime. In December 1997 *The Stage* newspaper reported that Peggy had withdrawn from her scheduled appearance as the Empress in *Aladdin* at the Hackney Empire (a part especially written for her) due to 'illness'. A spokeswoman for the show said, 'She's an elderly lady, and she's rather poorly. Obviously, we are all fingers crossed that she'll be back soon.'[271] It was with this simple statement that Peggy's fifty-year career finally came to an end.

Having experienced difficulties with her sight for decades, Peggy faced blindness with admirable courage. Ian Talbot remembers: 'She was very brave about it, so stoic.' Having known Peggy for many years before her sight finally failed, Ian admits: 'I knew she would go blind. Her eyesight had started to deteriorate and she tried to keep working, but she found it really hard. I think in the end it was total loss of vision; but there was no feeling of self-pity.'[272] Georgina Moon, who still occasionally saw Peggy socially, recalls that her former colleague 'handled it as best she could'[273] while Eira Griffiths admits that Peggy coped so well with the problem that at times it was easy to forget how poor her sight was: 'We were never conscious of her blindness. She had a reality and focus about her still; we tended to encourage her that she still belonged. She could act her way out of it when she was with people, but it was sad.'[274] At this crucial time, even more so than in the past, Eira would prove to be a vital support to Peggy and was, in the words of Ian Talbot, 'magnificent' in her care for her old friend.[275]

It was Eira who summed up the impact blindness had on Peggy's career:

Physically towards the end she was a professional and she would do anything to hide the deterioration that she had no control over, and yet she did have control because she knew what she had to project. She didn't hide behind her frailty – she couldn't absorb that in her mind… She overcame things and people respected her for that. It was sad in the end.[276]

The disability – and her subsequent reliance on others – also slightly mellowed Peggy; although many would argue to what extent (her final years in Denville Hall proved she had lost none of her feistiness). It appeared to make her appreciate the 'kindness' of those around her who were only too happy to help a now frail old lady. This was especially evident to Ian Talbot when Peggy continued to visit the Open Air Theatre, as she always had done, to support his events. Despite her affliction Peggy felt there was no reason why she shouldn't attend events and, as Ian remembers, 'She would always come to press nights; even when her sight was failing she would still turn up and she would give me a critique of what she thought of it. She was always absolutely charming with the public and I think when she lost her sight and people came up to her and still remembered her it really thrilled her.'[277] Mark Curry, on the other hand, felt that Peggy's loss of sight led to her feeling 'insecure' especially 'when meeting new people such as fans'.[278]

Peggy's loss of sight did not prevent her from bravely walking unaided to greet her old friend and one-time understudy Chili Bouchier for her 1996 *This Is Your Life* appearance. In the same year she was present at the unveiling of a Comic Heritage Blue Plaque in memory of her colleague Terry-Thomas outside 11 Queen's Gate Mews, Kensington (where he had lived from 1949 until 1981). Also featured among Peggy's latter public appearances were events such as Variety Club's celebration of Eric Sykes's fifty-year career in the summer of 1997, where she was able to mingle with numerous other stars including Sir John Mills (himself then almost blind at the age of eighty-nine), Michael Denison and his wife Dulcie Gray, David Lodge, Graham Stark, Ken Dodd, Spike Milligan and the sitcom writer Johnny Speight. Peggy also remained an active supporter of actors' rights and continued to attend Equity events, often accompanied by Eira Griffiths.

Peggy remained vigilant in attending many charity events where she revelled in encountering former colleagues. Jeffrey Holland would remember: 'We met her at various charity bashes with Patty Coombs, who she used to go around with a lot, and Patty used to push her in a wheelchair. We used to think, oh dear; but it comes to us all... I'd go up to her and say, "Hello Peggy, how are you?" and she would say, "Who's that?" because of course she couldn't see... I'd say, "It's Jeffrey Holland," and she'd say, "Oh, hello darling."'[279]

In 1998, at the age of eighty-three, Peggy made her final television appearance and could be seen sitting at a table in the audience of *In the Presence of Julian Clary*. In close proximity to various other thespians and accompanied by Eira (Griffiths) and Harry Darton, initially Peggy was seen wearing large wrap-around sunglasses to protect her eyes from the harsh studio lights, but these were quickly removed when she realised cameras were close by. Clary later admitted he got Peggy on the show because he had always loved her 'as a fellow eccentric English performer';[280] his camp humour clearly appealed to Peggy and she was seen looking amused and animated in several shots of the fifty-minute special. Halfway through the performance Clary would ask, 'Was that your tummy rumbling, Peggy Mount? Or was it an underground train?' much to Peggy's amusement. He then went on to say with heartfelt sincerity, 'I'm *so* thrilled you're here, Peggy,' before asking if Peggy would shout at him. A slightly bemused Peggy replied, 'I haven't shouted for years,' before booming out 'Julian!' in her typical fashion and to the delight of Clary and his audience. A satisfied Julian Clary thanked Peggy by saying, 'That's all I want,' to which Peggy quipped, 'That's all you're going to get.' It was a brief but touching appearance. The evening also provided Peggy with the opportunity to catch up with many show-business chums and colleagues including June Whitfield, Barbara Windsor, Frank Thornton, Dora Bryan and Fenella Fielding.

Of these final years Eira Griffiths would again reiterate how much Peggy's career had meant to her and how she happily became absorbed into their family life:

> In a strange sort of way acting was a protection cloak for her... Her life was her career – that was when she was a person who had an identity. The reality of her life and the non-existence of family meant we were family to her and she became part of us. She wasn't the actress Peggy Mount all the time – she was a real person and part of our family life. One never thought of her as a formidable star. She was quite a vulnerable lady and I think her relationship with us and our family was that she could be herself... almost rediscovering who she was: not the star – although that was something she was proud of and it gave her an identity – but I also think she would have liked children and a family life, so she enjoyed being with our children when they were growing up. She was part of our lives without being a star.[281]

8
Slow curtain…

'It was the perfect setting'

WITH THE LOSS OF her sight, and realising that the everyday tasks of life were becoming ever more difficult to cope with, Peggy made the decision to sell her home in London and move into Denville Hall, the actors' retirement home in Northwood, Middlesex. In her typically practical way Peggy was philosophical about the move into Denville and also 'ruthless' in clearing her home of personal possessions. As a result, many items of memorabilia and any personal records of her long and successful career were sadly seemingly lost forever. Rational as ever, Peggy perhaps realised she had no need to hang on to items that she could no longer properly see and fully appreciate – although, given her extremely private nature, her ruthlessness may also have been a deliberate attempt to leave behind as little personal

memorabilia as possible. Meanwhile her one-bedroom flat at
19 Devonia Road, Islington sold in June 1999 for £235,000.
Harry Darton, who oversaw Peggy's accounts in her latter
years, was able to take care of practical matters, and his wife
Eira carried out Peggy's request that items of furniture and
jewellery were sold at auction to contribute towards paying her
not inconsiderable nursing-home fees.

With its luxurious theatrical atmosphere, Denville Hall has
been a popular choice for many ageing actors over the years.
Arnold Ridley, best known as Private Godfrey in television's
Dad's Army, would spend his final days at the home and his
widow, Althea Ridley (1911-2001), was also a resident at the
same time as Peggy. Their son, Nicolas, would describe the
setting in his 2009 biography of his father:

> Denville Hall, the home for retired theatricals in Northwood, is a
> comfortable, caring place where actors end their days in the
> company of colleagues who have shared the life of the theatre. Plush
> carpeting, fresh flowers and polished furniture. Playbills and
> portraits, photographs and busts; venerable shadows, worthy props.
> An interval in which to rehearse and reminisce. A well-stocked bar
> which opens at lunchtime and again in the evening.[282]

Other opinions of the place differ and not everyone is
enamoured of its charms, with one source in the acting
profession admitting, 'I would seriously rather be dead than go
to Denville Hall. I think it's a hellhole beyond all measure. I
loathe it and it's exorbitantly expensive!'[283]

Thankfully, Peggy found herself very happy in her new
environment. Eira Griffiths described Denville Hall as the
'perfect setting' for Peggy during the final stage of her life:
'That's where she felt she needed to be – Denville – and we

made quite sure that she had things she treasured, like her clothes. She had no sentiment about possessions, but her face lit up when we took some of her things in.'[284] The privacy and safety of the residential home also appealed to Peggy, as Eira explains: 'She was desperately aware of her vulnerability in that it was something she couldn't change – she knew there was a deterioration… It was a vulnerability that she couldn't tackle; she couldn't command, she couldn't boom out any more… Denville was a kind of cloak…'[285]

Peggy would often see her friends privately in her own room, but did enjoy spending time in the Hall's lounge and bar where she was in the company of many well-known actors, who around that time included Maurice Denham, Doris Hare, Rose Hill, Sheila Keith, Elisabeth Welch and Anthony Steel. The atmosphere of the home suited many of its residents, although over the years there have been occasional moments when shock waves have rippled through its corridors. Betty Marsden, best known for her work on radio in *Round the Horne* and *Beyond Our Ken*, famously collapsed and died at Denville while enjoying a drink with friends in the summer of 1998; and inevitable clashes of personality between residents have occurred from time to time. Pat Coombs, for example, confided to the author that Anthony Steel took an instant dislike to her and ended up 'truly hating' her, telling her on one occasion that she looked like 'a third-rate brothel-keeper'.[286]

For Peggy there were frequent phone calls to and from friends with titbits and gossip about theatrical life. Ian Talbot recalls that she was warned at Denville not to pick anyone up if they fell because if she in turn fell 'they wouldn't be able to pick *her* up because of her weight'. Showing that she 'never lost her sense of humour', Peggy's response to this was, 'Well, I won't pick them up because I won't be able to bleeding well see them.'[287] Her most frequent visitor was Eira Griffiths who visited two or three times a week to spend time with her old friend and colleague.

Writer Pam Valentine had kept in touch with Pat Coombs since their years of working together on *You're Only Young Twice* and looked forward to Patty's regular phone calls. On Peggy's final years in Denville she recalls:

> It was terribly sad that she suffered from poor health and went blind, but of course she was very lucky to continue working for as long as she did and to earn the money she did… According to Patty, Peggy really was in charge of the other ladies in Denville. If she thought they were talking too much she would say 'Shut up'… Possibly she was a touch senile.[288]

While, according to those closest to her, Peggy's mental powers and particularly her ability to recall names remained undimmed even at the end of her life, it was certain that she was a formidable presence in the actors' retirement home. While many, including Georgina Moon, didn't realise Peggy had made the move to Denville, others such as Ayshea Brough assumed it was 'because she wanted the company', despite having lived alone for her entire adult life.[289]

Age, illness and infirmity did not keep Peggy out of the public eye completely. Never vain, she had no intentions of becoming a recluse in her eighties and thus continued to attend charitable functions and show-business events for as long as she could. On 26th June 1999 Pat Coombs would write to the author:

> Had a good night out last Sunday with Peg Mount – a showbiz 'do'
> at the Hilton Hotel given as a tribute to Ernie Wise – sad reason, but
> a sea of famous and familiar faces… so you can imagine all the gossip
> and 'get togethering' we enjoyed.[290]

It was during this time that Pat even had thoughts of reuniting with Peggy on television in new episodes of *You're Only Young Twice*. It would have been interesting to see how such a series would have been received although, alas, it was to be a 'pipe dream' and, as Pat Coombs admitted to the author, in light of the combined health problems of both ladies, 'The insurance on us both would go through the ceiling.'[291]

Many old friends and colleagues encountered Peggy during her final years, including Jean Bayliss. The pair had not met since their time together in *Humpty Dumpty* but, as Jean recalled, they would happily reunite at a party 'when Peggy had lost her sight'. They hugged each other and remembered that particularly happy time in both of their lives. Zulema Dene, who worked with Peggy on television in both *George and the Dragon* and *John Brown's Body*, also encountered her former colleague at the theatre. By this time Peggy made no secret of her life-changing condition and was 'upset' that her 'sight was going and that she was not going to be able to work'.[292]

Despite her blindness and growing frailty Peggy was encouraged to take once more to the stage for charity (namely the National Animal Welfare Trust) and agreed to take part in *An Audience with Peggy Mount and Pat Coombs*. The event, which was scheduled to take place at the Watermill Theatre in Newbury, on Sunday 24th October 1999, was to be hosted by actress Jean Fergusson, and Peggy and Pat Coombs would be on stage to recall their careers with 'sketches and anecdotes'.

Alas this final appearance did not come about. At the beginning of September 1999, by which time she was well settled in to Denville Hall, Peggy suffered the first of several minor strokes. In retrospect she was perhaps ideally placed to receive immediate medical attention. Pat Coombs informed the author of Peggy's illness on 29th September 1999:

> Poor Peggy Mount had a stroke a couple of weeks ago and was whipped into a hospital. We think and hope that it was a minor affair, but of all things, her speech has been badly affected, plus trouble with the right hand and other nasties like trouble with swallowing. Latest news is that she will be back 'home' on Thursday and will have daily speech therapy etc.

On 28th October 1999 Pat Coombs again wrote to the author regarding Peggy's recovery and dominance in the residential home:

> Elspeth March was very much the 'Queen' there and we think Peg M. is stepping into that vacancy!! Bless her – she is recovering well – still fumbling with words and, alas, her right hand is proving difficult to manoeuvre – but, with daily therapy, she is really making progress.

Although, as Eira Griffiths points out, Peggy's initial stroke was 'almost undetectable', it did cause limitations.[293] Naturally Peggy was unable to take part fully in the 'audience with' event at the Watermill Theatre, but less than two months after her stroke she was at least well enough to attend the event and sat in the front row of the audience. Despite their earlier encounter Jean Fergusson admits she did not know Peggy well enough to ask detailed questions on her career, but friends of Peggy were available to give her several questions to which Peggy could respond. After the event Peggy was photographed seated with Pat Coombs, Jean Fergusson and representatives from NAWT. Peggy was seen clutching a surgical walking stick in the photograph, oblivious to the attentions of the cameraman, and Pat Coombs later questioned: 'Why do we look so glum?' Always conscious of her size, Peggy had now shed a good deal of weight and her once rounded cheeks had noticeably lost their fullness in recent years. The event proved to be a big hit with the audience, and fundraiser Tony Readwin recalled the evening as a 'great success'.

Sadly health issues and increasing physical infirmity began to dominate Peggy's life. On 7th December 1999 Pat Coombs would write:

> Peg is recovering well... but her intolerant attitude towards some of the inmates is so unkind and doing her no good at all. Typical Peg, and has been ever since I knew her... silly, 'cos we all feel she is walking into another stroke.

Four months later, another update showed that Peggy's temper could still be as volatile as ever:

> Am doing the usual daily activities... local shops – Denville in the evening – tho' thanks to Peg's intolerance (and alas, jealousy) the last two visits have been tricky... She stomped angrily out of the bar on Monday saying (in THAT voice) 'I'm sick of seeing the back of you!!' just because I listen and chat to the others. It's norty isn't it?! And last night I never saw her at all... Everyone says, 'O! Forget it and let her get on with it,' but not so easy, is it? It'll blow over, I'm sure – but when *she's* ready!!![294]

The passage of time also, inevitably, meant the loss of many old friends and colleagues. The obituary columns throughout the 1990s and beyond were full of familiar names: Frankie Howerd, Bernard Bresslaw, Beryl Reid, Patrick Cargill, Hazel Bainbridge, Harry Secombe, to name but a few. Peggy was especially shocked to hear of the death of Chili Bouchier in September 1999, just three days before her ninetieth birthday. Having fallen on hard times Chili ended her days, reportedly drinking heavily, in a tiny ground-floor council flat in Marylebone where she was found dead after falling and hitting her head on a radiator.

Many of Peggy's final public appearances were at events to celebrate the lives of former colleagues and friends. Often accompanied by Pat Coombs or Eira Griffiths, Peggy enjoyed the camaraderie of these occasions and, even when her eyesight had failed, would make a determined effort to attend such functions. She was photographed being greeted by Peter O'Toole at one such event at the end of 1998, and in the spring of 2000 was well enough to attend the unveiling of a Comic Heritage Blue Plaque at the London Palladium in memory of Lord (Lew) Grade. The event, which included a lunch at the Hilton Park Hotel in London, was hosted by Tom O'Connor and attended by an array of well-known names including Norman Wisdom, Jack Douglas and John Inman.

With daily physiotherapy, the effects of Peggy's stroke were gradually reduced and by the summer of 2000 Pat Coombs wrote: 'Peg M well back to her normal intolerant self.'[295] Sadly that summer Peggy suffered a fall which naturally affected her confidence, leaving her increasingly reliant on others in order to move around. On 16th August Pat Coombs would write: 'Peg is recovering from her fall – but sort of frightened to move about without help (always at hand!). I've been driving again and popping out to local P.O. etc. so at the moment all's well.' By this stage Pat Coombs had also, happily, become a resident at Denville Hall. The idea of life imitating art has not been overlooked and many who knew Peggy and Pat felt it ironic that they should end up in a nursing home together, albeit a luxurious and well-respected establishment. It is easy to imagine the two ladies morphing into the characters they had once played in *You're Only Young Twice.*

Penny Hey, a niece of Pat's, revealed to the author some of her aunt's antics which mirrored slightly the mischievous behaviour of her on-screen character:

> She chose Denville as she had got to know it from visiting Peggy there and I do remember Pat got a telling off as some of the other residents would ask her to buy booze for them when she went there to visit Peggy and of course she did buy it. There was/is a bar there but I think the carers were unable to monitor alcohol intake and some of the residents were on a lot of medication.[296]

Pat Coombs's own health problems began in 1997 when she was diagnosed with osteoporosis. A lifelong heavy smoker, she also suffered from 'asthma' (later revealed as emphysema) and, despite her ever-cheerful persona, spent the last years of her life in constant pain as brittle bone disease gradually ravaged her body and saw her lose inches in height. Pat would later become involved with the National Osteoporosis Society, admitting her thrill at meeting the future Duchess of Cornwall (then Mrs Camilla Parker Bowles), whose mother had also suffered from the disease, and helping to raise £100,000 for the charity's Christmas appeal.

Almost inadvertently, a tremendous insight into Peggy's personality and activities in the final stage of her life was given to the author via letters from Pat Coombs. After becoming a permanent resident at Denville Hall in the summer of 2000 she penned a poem commemorating her move to the actors' retirement home, a handwritten copy of which she sent to the author:

'To Denville'

Denville 'All – up Northwood!
The place I wanted to be!
I'd passed the audition earlier
With a fag and a cuppa tea!

Now here I am all sorted
And settling in really well!
A lovely room with a magic bed *(an 'adjustable', Andrew!)*
And already stories to tell!

The smiling staff – my many pals –
Little bird in a cage 'n' all!
Then 'four paws Meg' the dog comes in
What's left? We can have a ball!

Just one little hiccup to worry –
My beloved 'Nola' the cat
But she's OK in a new home too
So that's the end of that!

Twice a day the bar's open
Twice a day we get drunk!
But no one as yet has been banished
And no one has done a bunk!

We laugh and enjoy the memories
Of wonderful times gone by
And tho' we fumble for names and stuff
We end the day with a sigh…
Of relief and joy at where we are
And we know we are here to stay
The end of our time –
What more is there left to say?

I hope you all will tolerate
My funny ways and such!
I'll try to be a good girl
'Cos I love it all so much!

Bless you Denville – and thank you all for such a wondrous curtain call!

Pat Coombs, Summer 2000

Pat Coombs gave a final update on Peggy's health (and temperament) following her fall on 2nd September 2000: 'She [Peggy] did recover very quickly and nothing was broken – but I think she lost confidence and was a bit afraid to walk without help… but she's fine once more and her usual, slightly difficult, self!!'

I last saw Patty Coombs in February 2001 following a recording *of Like They've Never Been Gone* at Broadcasting House in London. She sat waiting for me on the stage, propped up by a large cushion, until the audience had departed and I was escorted to her by a member of staff. Now tiny, painfully thin and increasingly frail, she nevertheless sparkled with life and wit and greeted me with an affectionate kiss directly on the lips – no showbiz 'air kisses' for this lady, I remember thinking at the time. We moved backstage for a buffet and champagne and I was introduced to the legendary Dame June Whitfield (and her daughter, actress Suzy Aitchison) and the delightful Roy Hudd and his charming wife, Debbie Flitcroft. Patty was full of chatter and clearly on a high following her live performance. On this occasion the redoubtable Peggy was not mentioned.

It was clear from Patty's letters and notes that Peggy's temperament at Denville Hall was not helped by her disability and the gradual indignities of extreme old age. Having always been physically strong and highly independent, the loss of her sight followed by the loss of her mobility hit Peggy hard. Her temper, not always restrained at the best of times, became especially short at times in these final years as she struggled to deal with the hand life had dealt her.

Gradually, during the second half of 2001, Peggy's health began slowly and finally to deteriorate. Pat Coombs also began a prolonged decline at around the same time, although she remained optimistic and as cheerful as ever about her predicament.

It was during these months that Zulema Dene, visiting another friend at Denville Hall, once again encountered Peggy. She would remember, with sadness, this closing stage of Peggy's life:

> She was having lunch and was very depressed because she had lost her sight. I felt that Peggy, who had lived for her work, now felt there was nothing left for her. When I left Denville that day I felt immensely sad that this woman with such talent and drive was just waiting for death.[297]

Mark Curry, who by 2001 had been friends with Peggy for over a decade, also took time to visit his former colleague, recalling in 2018:

> I do remember Peggy being generally quite depressed at the end of her life when I visited her in Denville Hall. She so wanted to be back out there performing. Show business had been her life and she missed it tremendously. But despite this, she took great delight hearing what I was up to, saying, 'Make the most of every minute, Mark, because this is what you were born to do; give it all you've got.' I get really quite sad remembering that.[298]

As the weeks passed Peggy's condition did not improve. She became weaker and weaker, and eventually the indomitable star became bedridden. On 3rd November she had her Last Will and Testament altered, appointing a new firm of solicitors to carry out her final wishes. Since she was too frail even to sign the codicil, the changes were instead read to her and signed on Peggy's behalf by Harry Darton and two other independent witnesses from the staff at Denville Hall.

In her final days, suffering from bronchopneumonia and congestive cardiac failure, she slipped in and out of consciousness. During this concluding period of Peggy's life, Eira Griffiths rarely left her friend's side. Eira would recall: 'She was unconscious for a lot of the time, and I'm not sure she even knew I was there most of the time… but I didn't want her to be alone.' Laid in a hospital-style bed, with metal sides to prevent her from falling out, Peggy was 'uncharacteristically silent'.[299] Her unforgettable, celebrated and unmistakable voice had at last failed. In 2017 Eira would recall Peggy's final hours:

> I sat with her all night… One knew it was going to happen but I didn't want her to know, and somehow sitting there made me feel I was perhaps projecting to her hope or something, but she was a realist – a total realist. She just lay there. I remember when I left she turned her head to face me. I think she was aware I was there. The rail was up on her bed but I did stretch my hand over to her. I needed to feel she knew I was there. I knew it was the end. Curtain down.[300]

During this final evening of Peggy's life, as she slept peacefully, Eira stayed with her friend until about midnight. A few hours later, in the early hours of 13th November, the Dartons received a telephone call from Denville Hall informing them that Peggy had died quietly in her sleep.

Summing up Peggy's final years Eira Griffiths would write:

The final exit of hers she timed to suit herself. There was no director
to say 'Go left' or 'Go right' or even 'Through the fireplace'.

Towards the end Peggy battled with lost eyesight, a pacemaker,
two hip replacements and then two strokes that robbed her of that
famous voice. It was time to go.[301]

Obituaries for Peggy quickly came flooding in. The BBC
website carried with it a selection of photographs of Britain's
most famous battleaxe: the beaming OBE investiture picture
and several later photographs, one taken shortly before Peggy's
death showing her looking much thinner, aged and unwell.
Although Peggy had disappeared from television screens in
the last few years of her career, and therefore slightly from
immediate public consciousness, without exception the tributes
were affectionate and praised the long and varied career of a
much-loved national institution.

Dennis Barker, writing for *The Guardian*, regarded her as
'the last of the time-honoured British battleaxes, equally at
home in the broadest of farces or in Brecht'[302] whilst the
Telegraph stated that she 'belonged to a hallowed tradition of
Amazonian scolds. She had teeth which gnashed whenever she
tried to smile, a gravelled voice which sounded like a cement
mixer, a broad beam and an even broader, scowl-ridden face'
while also praising her 'grotesquely comic harridans'.[303] Peggy
was rightly credited by *The Independent* as being one of
'television's biggest stars' for over twenty-five years[304] while
others labelled her quite simply as 'the last of the great British
dramatic battleaxes'.

If Peggy was indeed regarded as the ultimate British
'battleaxe' of stage and screen then she was by no means a mere

one-hit wonder. Her breadth of work in retrospect was truly diverse, and in some ways she was a forerunner to the many actresses who would follow in her footsteps. The likes of *Carry On* star Hattie Jacques and Violet Carson (best known as Ena Sharples in *Coronation Street*) were pigeon-holed into 'set' personas and arguably fixed in the minds of television viewers as one character. Whilst the image of a strong, powerful woman never left her, Peggy's public image was slightly more fluid than many of her contemporaries and this allowed her to take on a great variety of roles, especially on stage.

As a person Peggy was equally fluid and complex. Her outward exterior of matronly homeliness suited the image of a lady who was at her happiest knitting, gardening or cooking; yet she was also fiercely independent, intensely proud, solitary and occasionally downright aloof. At times she enjoyed the company of friends and the comfortable atmosphere of family life; yet her own family and her closest living relative, in the form of her only sister, were obliterated from her life. Such paradoxes are slightly difficult to weigh up, yet it is worth remembering that, for all her human foibles, Peggy was truly loved and admired by friends and colleagues alike, and this is surely how she should be remembered.

Ayshea Brough is one of many in the profession who remain fulsome in their praise of Peggy's career and professionalism:

Peggy was someone who had achieved so much; similar to Patricia Routledge: a really accomplished actress who was fabulous at comedy. She's in the school of Joyce Grenfell and Margaret Rutherford. They never played on beauty. They were women who were incredible and often did roles in TV shows that a man would have done. I thought she was great and I don't say that lightly. I've worked with so many people, and you can meet people who have been so successful but then they have so many issues and can be so difficult, and she was just as easy as it comes. I never heard her say a word to complain – she would do her job and that was it.[305]

Christopher Biggins would write: 'It was such a pleasure to work with her and have been touched by the greatness of such a wonderful woman; I have many happy memories of Peg.'[306] Director Bill Bryden tenderly admits: 'Her wit, talent and personality are sorely missed.'[307]

Friend and colleague Mark Curry adored Peggy, as he revealed to the author in 2018:

Peggy Mount is a comedy legend I think. There has never been a stronger 'dragon', in my opinion. Her vocal strength when belting out an angry line was amazing. She was totally focused when she was acting: no distractions, solid, powerful and a total professional with great comedy timing. Peggy was around when most of the leading comic actors were male, but she could hold her own with any of them (with Sid James in *George and the Dragon*, for example). Peggy was above all a good actress who played the reality of the comedic situations, not just going for the laughs. It's important that we remember her and what she achieved, because she really was a star who never stopped working until her health failed her. Her career was *so* successful, embracing theatre, television and film. She made a lot of money too! I'm so proud to have worked with her and she became a great friend.[308]

Writer Pam Valentine perhaps summed up Peggy's life in the kind of matter-of-fact way that would have suited the lady herself, feeling that on the whole Peggy 'had a bloody good life: she was successful, she earned money, she had friends when she needed them and was looked after to the end'.[309]

Six days after Peggy's death, on the afternoon of Monday 19th November 2001, a service of thanksgiving and celebration for her life took place at Breakspear Crematorium in Ruislip.

Led by the Reverend David Dickinson of Northwood Method-ist Church, the service began with the overture from *Romeo and Juliet*, and included a gospel reading, two songs from Peggy's 1996 *Desert Island Discs* appearance (*Say it with Flowers* and *Portrait of My Love*) and the following tribute from Eira Griffiths-Darton:

'Let's all go down the Strand'

In 1955 everyone was going down the Strand to see Peggy Mount in *Sailor, Beware!* at the Strand Theatre.

Peggy herself, on the second night after opening, cowered in a shop doorway near the theatre, not quite believing her name was up in lights above the title.

In later years she said that *Sailor, Beware!* gave her everything she ever wanted. When she turned up at the Caprice armed with a net bag containing a cabbage and onions – and she did, just once – Mario discreetly took the bag and, all smiles, ushered her to the best table.

A star was born – and now has died.

In a long career she 'strutted the stage like a colossus' and was on home ground every time she walked through a stage door anywhere in the world.

'I'll never work again' was a familiar mantra from Peggy whenever a job finished. The resting periods were, however, very few, and a long career playing many notable parts gave the lie in her case to what is, after all, every actor's nightmare. Theatre, films, television, radio... she enjoyed great success in all the media and it is safe to say that her audiences were never short-changed.

Her friends were never short-changed either. Mind you, she could ground you with a look or a flounce if something displeased her, but her friendship was always something to be valued. There are not many who have not possessed and worn something she has knitted. There are many cold feet that have been warmed by her knitted slippers. Who has not enjoyed the home-made marmalade, the annual Christmas puddings and the wonderful steak and kidney puddings? Who has not seen her get out her personal supply of tea bags to strengthen up the tea served in cafes and hotels all round the country? And there cannot be many who do not have in their gardens a plant she has nurtured.

This star has not died. She is around in so many ways.

'I will not say the day is done nor bid farewell to the stars'[310]

While never especially religious, Peggy was brought up as a Methodist and even signed the pledge, so the setting for her funeral was appropriate. Not surprisingly Nancy Mount, then almost ninety years old but in good health, did not attend the event. A remembrance service was also later held at Denville Hall where everyone reflected on her life and career and her favourite songs were again played. Peggy had become one of Denville's most memorable characters and, as Eira Griffiths recalled, 'She wasn't ever really going to disappear – there was great affection for her.'[311]

In her Last Will and Testament Peggy left her personal chattels to Eira Griffiths, and her monetary estate (valued at £353,278 gross and £351,406 after taxes, the bulk of which had come from the sale of her London home), was divided equally between Eira and Harry Darton and Michael Evans and his sons (upon their attaining the age of twenty-one). This considerable sum was a testament to Peggy's hard work throughout her long career and careful management of money. Despite her wealth, and very occasional extravagances, she had always remained conscious of her humble origins and the financial hardships she had faced from childhood until achieving stardom in her forties. It is fair to say that Peggy's careful lifestyle meant that she ended her days considerably wealthier than many of her contemporaries.

A final tribute to Peggy Mount came on 19th June 2002 when, after a special performance of *Romeo and Juliet*, glasses of champagne were raised in her memory and her ashes were scattered by Ian Talbot in the grounds of the Open Air Theatre in Regent's Park, in the presence of about twenty close friends. Peggy's life had undoubtedly been devoted to the theatre and entertainment and in this capacity she brought joy to millions of lives. She was at her happiest whilst performing, especially on stage, and indomitably continued to work for as long as she was physically able. The profession she so dearly loved had arguably given her everything she had ever wanted. It would seem fitting that in the end she should return, in death, to a place she had so dearly loved in life. She had indeed come home.

Stage credits

Include:

Studied for the stage privately under Phyllis Reader and made
her first stage appearances in wartime concert parties.
Received the Gold Medal for elocution (17 and over category,
Southend Music Festival, November 1938).

1939-45: performed at numerous concerts during World War
II and worked with ENSA.

1944: *Hindle Wakes* (Hippodrome, Keighley, as Mrs
    Hawthorne)

Additional (undated) repertory appearances:

Relative Values (as Moxie)
Waters of the Moon (as Mrs Ashworth)
Ring Round the Moon (as Madam Devin)
Murder Mistaken (as Freda)
The Hollow (as Lady Angkatell)

The River Line (as Mrs Mirivan)
Saloon Bar (as Charwoman)
Shop at Sly Corner (as Mrs Katt)
Double Door (as Victoria)
I Lived With You (as Cockney Mother)
Don't Listen Ladies (as Julie Bien Bois)
Caesar and Cleopatra (as Ftatateeta)
The Brothers Castiglioni (as Italian Mother)

1945-48: performed with the Harry Hanson Court Players, including:

1945: *Paddy the Next Best Thing* (Prince's Theatre, Bradford, as Miss O'Hara, with Cissie Ashley)
1945: *Nothing But the Truth* (as Ethel, Royalty Theatre, Chester)
1945: *The Barretts of Wimpole Street* (as Arabel Barrett)
1945: *The Best People* (as Miss Tate)
1945: *Indian Summer* (as Kitty)
1946: *The Barretts of Wimpole Street* (Prince's Theatre, Bradford)
1946: *Paddy the Next Best Thing* (Prince's Theatre, Bradford)
1946: *Murder Out of Tune* (Theatre Royal, Leeds)
1946: *George and Margaret* (Theatre Royal, Leeds)
1946: *Potiphar's Wife* (Theatre Royal, Leeds)

1948-54: performed in repertory at Colchester, Preston, Dundee, Wolverhampton and Liverpool, including:

1949: *The House of Women* (Dundee Repertory Theatre, as Aunt Hatty)
1949: *Yes and No* (Dundee)

1949: *Wuthering Heights* (Dundee)

1949: *The Circle* (Beach Pavilion, as Lady Kitty)

1949: *Love in Idleness* (Hippodrome, Preston)

1949: *The Night of January 16* (Hippodrome, Preston)

1949: *While Parents Sleep* (Hippodrome, Preston, as Nanny)

1950: *The Foolish Gentlewoman* (Cheltenham Opera House)

1950: *The Brothers Castiglioni* (Liverpool Playhouse, as Eusabia)

1950: *The Blue Goose* (Grand Theatre, Wolverhampton)

1951: *The Young in Heart* (Royal Hippodrome, Preston, as Margaret Purvis)

1952: *Johnny Belinda* (Grand Theatre, Wolverhampton)

1951: *Humpty Dumpty* (Pantomime, at the London Palladium, as the Witch, with Norman Evans, Terry-Thomas, Gillian Lynne, Noele Gordon)

1953: *The Sleeping Beauty* (Wolverhampton, as the Witch)

1954: *Sailor, Beware!* (Connaught, Worthing)

1954: *Because I am Black* (Connaught, Worthing)

1954: *Beside the Seaside* (Connaught, Worthing)

1955-57: *Sailor, Beware!* (over 1,000 performances at the Strand Theatre, as Emma Hornett)

1957: *Man on Trial* (Lyric, for the Repertory Players, as the Charwoman)

1958: *The Importance of Being Earnest* (Salisbury, as Lady Bracknell)

1959: *Farewell, Farewell, Eugene* (Grand Theatre, Leeds, and Garrick, as Florence Povis, with Margaret Rutherford)

1960: *Romeo and Juliet* (Old Vic, as the Nurse)

1960: *She Stoops to Conquer* (Old Vic, as Mrs Hardcastle)

1962: *All Things Bright and Beautiful* (Bristol Old Vic and Phoenix, London, as Queenie Hesseltine)

1964: Tribute to Michael Holliday (Prince of Wales Theatre, special event featuring Matt Monro, Bruce Forsyth, Frankie Howerd, Benny Hill, Max Bygraves, Alma Cogan, Dorothy Squires)

1964: *Mother's Boy* (Globe and The Royal, Brighton, as Mrs Spicer, with David Tomlinson)

1964: *The Beaver Coat* (Arts, Ipswich, as Mrs Wolff)

1965: *Did You Feel It Move?* (Alexandra, Birmingham, as Gladys)

1966: *What About Stanley?* (Alexandra, Birmingham, as Gracie Plimmer)

1966: *The Beaver Coat* (Mermaid, as Mrs Wolff)

1968: *Oh Clarence!* (Lyric, as Dame Daphne Winkworth)

1969: *The Bandwagon* (Mermaid, as Mrs Botterill)

1969: *When We Are Married* (Marlowe, Canterbury, as Clara Soppitt)

1970: *The Bandwagon* (Australian tour)

1970: *When We Are Married* (Arnaud, Guilford and the Strand, as Clara Soppitt)

1971: *The Rivals* (as Mrs Malaprop, Lanchester Arts Festival/Coventry Belgrade Company)

1971: *Sailor, Beware!* (as Emma Hornett, Ashcroft, Croydon and Richmond)

1971-72: *Alice in Wonderland* (Royal Shakespeare Company, Stratford-upon-Avon)

1972: *The Circle* (as Lady Catherine Champion Cheney, Forum, Billingham)

1973: *Jack and Knaves* (Palace, Westcliff)

1973: *Alice In Wonderland* (Theatre Royal, Brighton, with Marianne Faithfull)

1973: *All Things Bright and Beautiful* (Leigh-on-Sea and tour, as Queenie Hesseltine)

1974: *There Goes the Bride* (Criterion Theatre, as Daphne Drimmond, with Bernard Cribbins, Terence Alexander, Jane Downs, Bill Pertwee)

1974: *Water, Water Everywhere* (Brighton Festival – Pavilion, Brighton, with Peter Wyngarde, Peter Gilmore and John Gould)

1974: *The Confederacy* (Chichester Festival, as Mrs Amlet)

1975: *The Anniversary* (Everyman Theatre, Cheltenham)

1976: *II Campiello* (National Theatre, with Beryl Reid)

1976: *Signed and Sealed* (Comedy Theatre, with Kenneth Williams)

1977: *Porter Must Go* (Connaught, Worthing, with Hugh Lloyd and Vivienne Johnson)

1978: *Plunder* (National Theatre, as Mrs Hewlett)

1978: *Blithe Spirit* (Leigh-on-Sea)

1978: City of London Festival (guest appearance, Mermaid Theatre)

1979: *Rookery Nook* (with Nicky Henson, Terence Frisby, Gaye Brown, Andrew Robertson and Peter Schofield)

1979: *Candleford* (National Theatre)

1979: *Blithe Spirit* (Palace, Westcliff)

1980: *My Giddy Aunt* (Middle and Far East tour for Derek Nimmo)

1980: *Blithe Spirit* (Hong Kong tour for Derek Nimmo)

1981: *Mrs Tucker's Pageant* (Theatre Royal, Stratford East)

1981-82: *The Mating Game* (national tour, with Norman Vaughan, Barbara Windsor, Ann Sidney, Ian Masters)

1982: *Park Follies* (charity event at the Open Air Theatre, Regent's Park)

1982: *The Killing of Sister George* (Watermill Theatre)

1982: *Cinderella* (Theatre Royal, Bath, with Bill Owen, Jimmy Edwards, Brian Cant, Ann Sidney and Aimi MacDonald)

1983-85: With the Royal Shakespeare Company:
The Dillen, Measure for Measure, Mary After the Queen and *The Happiest Days of Your Life* (Stratford and tours)

1985: *The Good and Faithful Servant* (for the RSC, as Edith, The Other Place, Stratford-upon-Avon, directed by Ian Talbot)

1986-87: *Rookery Nook* (Shaftesbury Theatre, with Tom Courtenay)

1987: *Party Piece* (Thorndike Theatre)

1987: *Bartholomew Fair* (Open Air Theatre, Regent's Park, as Ursula)

1988: *Cinderella* (Manchester, as Fairy Godmother)

1989: *Blithe Spirit* (as Madame Arcati, Lyric, Hammersmith, Theatre Royal, Windsor, and tour)

1989: *Move Over Mrs Markham* (Churchill, Bromley)

1990: *Breath of Spring* (Churchill Theatre, Bromley, as Nan, with Georgina Cookson, Hazel Bainbridge, Jack Douglas and Barbara New)

1990: *A Touch of Mink*

1990-91: *Cinderella* (with Des O'Connor, Eric Sykes, The Simmons Brothers, David Morton and Brian Godfrey, Theatre Royal, Plymouth)

1992-93: *Pied Piper of Hamelin* (with Wayne Sleep and Richard Marner, Cliffs Pavilion, Southend-on-Sea)

1993: *The Happiest Days of Your Life* (Theatre Royal, Windsor)

1993-94: *Puss in Boots* (with Bob Carolgees and Liza Goddard, Lyceum Theatre, Crewe)

1994: *Dilemma for Murder* (Watermill, Newbury, as a guest celebrity)

1994-95: *Cinderella* (with Wayne Sleep, Christopher Beeny, Jayne Collins, Martina & Melanie Grant and Stephen J. Dean, Harlequin Theatre, Redhill)

1995-96: *Cinderella* (with Sonia, Wayne Sleep, Mike Holoway and John Challis, Lyceum Theatre, Crewe)

1996: Molière's *Tartuffe* (with Tom Hollander, Ian McDiarmid and Susannah Harker, directed by Jonathan Kent, Almeida)

1996: *Uncle Vanya* (as Marina, with Derek Jacobi, Albery Theatre)

1996-97: *Jack and the Beanstalk* (Towngate Theatre, Poole)

Film credits

1954

The Embezzler (as Mrs Larkin)
Director: John Gilling
Cast: Charles Victor, Zena Marshall, Avice Landone,
 Frank Forsyth, Leslie Weston, Michael Craig

1956

Sailor Beware! (as Emma Hornett) (US: *Panic in the Parlour*)
Director: Gordon Parry
Cast: Shirley Eaton, Ronald Lewis, Cyril Smith, Esma
 Cannon, Gordon Jackson, Geoffrey Keen, Joy Webster,
 Thora Hird, Eliot Makeham, Edie Martin

Dry Rot (as Sergeant Fire)
Director: Maurice Elvey
Cast: Ronald Shiner, Brian Rix, Sidney James, Michael Shepley,
 Joan Haythorne, Joan Sims, Heather Seers, Lee Patterson

1958

The Naked Truth (as Flora Ransom) (US: *Your Past is Showing*)
Director: Mario Zampi
Cast: Terry-Thomas, Peter Sellers, Shirley Eaton, Dennis
Price, Georgina Cookson, Joan Sims, Miles Malleson

1960

Inn For Trouble (as Ada Larkins)
Director: Pennington Richards (C. M. Pennington-Richards)
Cast: David Kossoff, Leslie Phillips, Glyn Owen, Charles
Hawtrey, A. E. Matthews, Yvonne Monlaur, Irene Handl

1963

Ladies Who Do (as Mrs Cragg)
Director: C. M. Pennington-Richards
Cast: Robert Morley, Harry H. Corbett, Miriam Karlin,
Avril Elgar, Dandy Nichols, Jon Pertwee, Ron Moody,
Cardew Robinson, John Laurie

1965

One Way Pendulum (as Mrs Myra Gantry)
Director: Peter Yates
Cast: Eric Sykes, George Cole, Julia Foster, Jonathan Miller,
Alison Leggatt, Mona Washbourne

1966

Hotel Paradiso (as Angelique Boniface)
Director: Peter Glenville
Cast: Gina Lollobrigida, Alec Guinness, Robert Morley,
Douglas Byng, Robertson Hare, Akim Tamiroff

Finders Keepers (as Mrs Bragg)
Director: Sidney Hayers
Cast: Cliff Richard, Brian Bennett, John Rostill,
    Robert Morley, Viviane Ventura, Graham Stark,
    John Le Mesurier, Robert Hutton

1968

Oliver! (as Mrs Bumble)
Director: Carol Reed
Cast: Ron Moody, Oliver Reed, Shani Wallis, Mark Lester,
    Jack Wild, Harry Secombe, Hugh Griffith, Hylda Baker,
    Megs Jenkins, Leonard Rossiter, Joseph O'Conor

1991

The Princess and the Goblin (voice only, as the Goblin Queen)
Director: József Gémes
Cast: Joss Ackland, Claire Bloom, Rik Mayall, Roy Kinnear,
    Sally Ann Marshall, Peter Murray, Mollie Sudgen,
    Victor Spinetti

Television credits

Include:

1953: *Fortune House* (as Aunt Sophia)

1953: *The Sleeping Beauty* (as the nurse)

1954: *The Windmill Family – Robinson Minor* (as Miss Skiffhampton)

1954: *The Cabin in the Clearing* (as Polly Sutherland)

1955: *Robinson and Co.* (as Mrs Cartwright)

1957: *Theatre Night – Sailor Beware* (as Emma Hornett)

1958: *The Adventures of Mr Pastry* (as Landlady)

1958: *ITV Play of the Week – Arsenic and Old Lace* (as Abby Brewster)

1958: *The Visit to Paradise Buildings* (as Mamma Decomano)

1958-64: *The Larkins* (6 series, 40 episodes, as Ada Larkins)

1961-62: *Winning Widows* (2 series, as Martha)

1965: *Comedy Playhouse – Mother Came Too* (as
   Mrs Preston, pilot with Graham Stark)

1966-68: *George and the Dragon* (4 series, as Gabrielle Dragon,
   with Sid James, John Le Mesurier and Keith Marsh)

1966: *The Tommy Steele Show – The Squire* (guest appearance)

1966: *Rome Sweet Home*

1968-69: *The Harry Secombe Show* (guest appearances)

1969: *John Browne's Body* (7 episodes, as Virginia Browne)

1969: *The Frankie Howerd Show* (guest appearance)

1972: *Lollipop* (2 series, 14 episodes, as Maggie Robinson)

1973: *Once Upon a Time* (as Proprietress, with Tommy Steele)

1973: *ITV Play of the Week – Queen of Hearts* (as Queen of
   Spades)

1973: *Quiet Waters* (with Deryck Guyler)

1976: *Spice Island, Farewell!* (with Peter Vaughan)

1976: *The Chiffy Kids* (guest appearance as Mrs Foster)

1976: *Just Like Mum* (as Mrs Jordan)

1977: *Mother Courage*

1977-81: *You're Only Young Twice* (4 series, 31 episodes, as
   Flora Petty)

1978: *Stargazy on Zummerdown* (as Opinionated Alice)

1981: *The End of the Pier Show* (as Mrs Pumphrey)

1984: *It's Never Too Late* (as Winifred Walker, with
    Pat Coombs, Hugh Lloyd and Harold Goodwin)

1986: *Twist in the Tale* (with Donald Pleasence)

1987: *Screenplay – The Trial of Klaus Barbie* (as Joly)

1988: *The Ray Bradbury Theatre – Punishment Without
    Crime* (as the Judge)

1989: *Doctor Who – The Greatest Show in the Galaxy*
    (2 episodes, as Stallslady)

1991: *All Change* (second series, as Aunt Fanny, with Frankie
    Howerd)

1991: *Inspector Morse – Fat Chance* (as nun)

1991: *Casualty – Sins of Omission* (as Eliza Johnstone)

1991: *T-Bag's Christmas Turkey* (as Mumsy Bag)

1992: *Virtual Murder – A Dream of Dracula* (as Mrs Weaver)

1994: *The Tomorrow People* (*The Monsoon Man: Part 2*, as
    Mrs Butterworth)

Additional appearances:

1956: *Film Fanfare* (as herself)

1956: *Mainly for Women: Twice Twenty* (as herself)

1960: *The Jack Paar Tonight Show*

1961/65: *Juke Box Jury* (as herself)

1970: *The Golden Shot* (as herself)

1976: *The Good Old Days*

1976: *Those Wonderful TV Times* (as herself)

1976: *Looks Familiar* (as herself)

1976: *Celebrity Squares* (with Bob Monkhouse, Pat Coombs, Clive Dunn, Doris Hare, Wendy Richard, Ray Alan)

1978: *Golden Gala* (as herself)

1979: *Tell Me Another* (5 episodes, as herself)

1979, 81-85: *Blankety Blank* (guest appearances, as herself)

1979: *Definition* (as herself, with Nicholas Parsons)

1980: *Cannon and Ball* (as herself and playing Mrs Jackson)

1980: *Night of a Thousand Stars*

1981: *Play School*

1981: *Larry Grayson's Generation Game*

1983: *Six Fifty-Five* (BBC 2 interview)

1984: *The Marti Caine Show*

1989: *Hudson and Halls*

1996: *This Is Your Life* (Chili Bouchier)

1998: *In the Presence of Julian Clary* (as herself)

Radio credits

Include:

1955: *All in the Day's Work* (interview)

1957: *Woman's Hour* (guest)

1959: *Britannia of Billingsgate*

1962: *Big Bertha* (Home Service, as Bertha Briggs)

1962: *In Town Today*

1965: *Alice in Wonderland* (edited version of LP)

1966: *She Stoops to Conquer* (World Service)

1967: *Home This Afternoon*

1968: *Galaxy* (Radio 1 and 2)

1968: *Desert Island Discs* (guest with Roy Plomley)

1968: *Million Dollar Bill* (Radio 2, guest)

1969: *A Choice of Paperbacks* (speaking about *Lord of the Rings*, Radio 4)

1969: *Pete's Saturday People* (Radio 1 and 2)

1969 & 70: *Open House* (Radio 2)

1970: *Cash at Four* (Radio 1)

1970-72: *Late Night Extra* (guest appearances)

1971: *Music For Sunday* (Radio 2)

1971 & 72: *Sounds Familiar* (Radio 2, guest)

1972: *The Silent Woman* (Radio 3)

1973-75: *Petticoat Line* (guest panellist)

1973: *The Bedsitter*

1974: *Does the Team Think* (Radio 4)

1975: *Pause for Thought* (Radio 2)

1975: *The Impresarios* (with Michael Craig and Evelyn Laye)

1976: *Open House* (Radio 2)

1976: *Jack de Manio Precisely* (interview)

1976: *Cheeky Whittington and his Magic Ballpoint* (with Tim Brooke-Taylor, Barry Cryer and John Junkin, Radio 2)

1978: *Open House* (Radio 2)

1978: *Dandy Dick* (Play of the Week)

1979: *Breakaway* (interview with Barry Norman)

1979: *The Late Show*

1979: *Listening and Writing*

1980: *Sailor, Beware!*

1982-83: *Funny You Should Ask* (Radio 2, guest appearances)

1983: *Blithe Spirit* (with Paul Eddington, Julia McKenzie and Anna Massey)

1983: *Morning Story* (Radio 4)

1984: *Bleak House* (as Mrs Guppy)

1984: *The Paul McDowell Show* (guest)

1984: *John Dunn – The Fosdyke Saga* (Radio 2, as the Tripe Inspector)

1984: *Railway Carriage Game*

1985: *The Old Ladies at the Zoo* (Radio 4, as Bruno, with Liz Smith)

1985: *The Fosdyke Saga II* (as the Tripe Inspector)

1986: *Inman and Friends* (guest)

1988: *The Christmas Jottings of Hinge and Bracket* (guest)

1996: *Secombe … So Far* (Radio 2)

1996: *Desert Island Discs* (guest with Sue Lawley)

Bibliography

Kaye Crawford, *Roll Out the Beryl! The Authorised Biography of Beryl Reid*, Fantom Publishing, 2016.

Davies, Russell (editor), *The Kenneth Williams Diaries*, HarperCollins *Publishers*, 1993.

Dunn, Kate, *Exit Through the Fireplace – The Great Days of Rep*, John Murray, 1998.

Hayward, Anthony, *Who's Who on Television*, Boxtree, 1990 & 1996.

Lewisohn, Mark, *Radio Times Guide to TV Comedy*, BBC Worldwide, 1998.

Lloyd, Hugh, *Thank God For a Funny Face*, John Blake, 2002.

Merriman, Andy, *Margaret Rutherford – Dreadnought with Good Manners,* Aurum Press, 2009.

Perry, Jimmy, *A Stupid Boy*, Century, 2002.

Reid, Beryl, *So Much Love*, Hutchinson, 1984.

Ridley, Nicolas, *Godfrey's Ghost – From Father to Son*, Mogzilla Life, 2009.

Stevens, Christopher, *Born Brilliant – The Life of Kenneth Williams*, John Murray (Publishers), 2010.

Stone, Richard, *You Should Have Been in Last Night*, The Book Guild Ltd, 2000.

Notes on the chapters

Chapter 1

[1] Peggy Mount was born at 70 Christchurch Road, Southend-on-Sea – a two-bedroom Victorian terrace property. At the time of her birth her father's occupation was listed as a grocer's assistant.

[2] Nancy Mount, BBC Radio interview, 1993. Tom Carney's son, Will (William), and daughter-in-law, Edith Shorey, were also well known in the world of local amusement.

[3] Nancy Mount, BBC Radio interview, 1993.

It was reported that Tom Carney's wife died in October 1910 in St Bartholomew's Hospital, Barnsbury, at the age of fifty-two. She was buried at Finchley Cemetery. Just over a year later, in December 1911, Tom Carney died suddenly at his home in Mesly Road, Barnsbury having been found dead in his bed by his twelve-year-old son, Ernest Stanley Penney. A post mortem later revealed the cause of death to be heart failure, following acute pneumonia, gastric catarrh and bronchitis.

It was reported in the press that he had been in 'his usual good health until a few days before his death, when he complained of being very ill. Although he had not appeared very happy of late, he had had all he wanted.' A verdict of death by 'natural causes' was returned by the jury following an inquest at Islington Coroner's Court. Source: *The Music Hall & Theatre Review*, 14th December 1911.

[4] Nancy discussed her mother's final appearance on BBC Radio in 1993 but appeared to confuse the date concerning the event. She stated that the event took place in 1960 when her mother was 'seventy-eight' and that it was in the year of her death. Rose Mount actually died in 1968, aged eighty-four.

[5] Peggy Mount, *Desert Island Discs* interview, 1996.

[6] Pam Valentine, interview with the author, 2017.

[7] Nancy Mount, BBC Radio interview, 1993.

[8] Nancy Mount, BBC Radio interview, 1993.

[9] Ayshea Brough, interview with the author, 2017.

[10] Mark Curry, email to the author, 2018.

[11] *Basildon Canvey Southend Echo*, 15th November 2001.

[12] Peggy Mount, *Desert Island Discs* interview, 1996.

[13] Peggy Mount, *Desert Island Discs* interview, 1996.

[14] *The Independent*, 14th November 2001.

[15] Peggy Mount, *Desert Island Discs* interview, 1996.

[16] Penny Ryder, interview with the author, 2017.

[17] Peggy Mount, *Desert Island Discs* interview, 1996.

[18] *The Essex Chronicle*, 4th June 1937.

[19] Mark Curry, email to the author, 2018.

Chapter 2

[20] *The Essex Chronicle*, 30th October 1942.

[21] Philip and Sally Brazier, email to the author, 2017.

[22] Lindsay Maggs, email to the author, 2017.

[23] Philip and Sally Brazier, email to the author, 2017.

24   *The Evening Echo*, 18th April 1978.

25   Eira Griffiths, interview with the author, 2017.

26   John Holmes, email to the author, 2017.

27   Mark Curry, email to the author, 2018.

28   Alan Bennett, letter to the author, 2017.

29   Eira Griffiths, interview with the author, 2017.

30   Peggy Mount, *Desert Island Discs* interview, 1996.

31   Ian Talbot, interview with the author, 2017.

32   Philip and Sally Brazier, email to the author, 2017.

33   Nick Corrigan, email to the author, 2017.

34   Philip and Sally Brazier, email to the author, 2017.

35   Joan & Harry Maggs (Lindsay Maggs), email to the author, 2017.

36   *Basildon Canvey Southend Echo*, 24th June 2011.

37   *Evening Echo*, 18th April 1978.

38   *Exit Through the Fireplace – The Great Days of Rep*, by Kate Dunn, pg. 55.

39   Peggy Mount, *Desert Island Discs* interview, 1996.

40   Jean Bayliss, letter to the author, 2017.

41   *The Stage*, 12th May 1955.

42   *Exit Through the Fireplace – The Great Days of Rep*, by Kate Dunn, pg. 19.

43   *Exit Through the Fireplace – The Great Days of Rep*, by Kate Dunn, pg. 223.

44   *Exit Through the Fireplace – The Great Days of Rep*, by Kate Dunn, pg. 133.

45   *The Stage*, 12th May 1955.

46   Peggy Mount, *Desert Island Discs* interview, 1996.

47   Peggy Mount, *Desert Island Discs* interview, 1996.

48   *The Stage*, 26th October, 1950.

49   Sir Ian McKellen, letter to the author, 2017.

50   *The Times*, 14th November 2001.

51   *The Guardian*, 14th November 2001.

52   Peggy Mount, *Desert Island Discs* interview, 1996.
53   Ayshea Brough, interview with the author, 2017.
54   Damaris Hayman, interview with the author, 2017.
55   Peggy Mount, *Desert Island Discs* interview, 1996.
56   Damaris Hayman, interview with the author, 2017.
57   John Standing, interview with the author, 2017.
58   Pam Valentine, interview with the author, 2017.
59   Penny Hey, email to the author, 2017.
60   Jeffrey Holland, interview with the author, 2017.
61   Ian Masters, interview with the author, 2018.
62   Claudia Mayer, interview with the author, 2018.
63   Eira Griffiths, interview with the author, 2017.
64   Mark Curry, email to the author, 2018.
65   Norman Newell outlived Peggy by three years. He retired in 2001 and died on 1st December 2004, following a series of debilitating strokes, aged eighty-five. He was awarded the OBE shortly before his death.
66   *The Express, The Express on Sunday*, 23rd April 2002.
67   Eira Griffiths, interview with the author, 2018.
68   Eira Griffiths, interview with the author, 2017.
69   Jeffrey Holland, interview with the author, 2017.
70   *The Stage*, 12th May 1955.
71   *Weekend*, 2-8 November 1977.
72   Peggy Mount, *Desert Island Discs* interview, 1996.
73   Mark Curry, email to the author, 2018.

Chapter 3

74   *The Stage*, 17th September 1953.
75   *The Stage*, 29th July 1954.
76   *The Herald*, 3rd December 1954.
77   *The Stage*, 12th May 1955.

[78]   *The Stage,* 24th February 1955.

[79]   *The Yorkshire Post and Leeds Mercury*, 18th February 1955.

[80]   *The Birmingham Post*, 18th February 1955.

[81]   Sir Ian McKellen, letter to the author, 2017.

[82]   Ian Talbot, interview with the author, 2017.

[83]   Mark Curry, email to the author, 2018.

[84]   *The Tatler and Bystander*, 2nd March 1955.

[85]   *The Tatler and Bystander*, 2nd March 1955.

[86]   *The Independent*, obituary notice by Anthony Hayward, 14th November 2001.

[87]   *Coventry Evening Telegraph TV Extra*, 16th June 1979.

[88]   Mark Curry, email to the author, 2018.

[89]   Eira Griffiths, interview with the author, 2018.

[90]   *The Stage*, 21st January 1960.

[91]   *The Stage,* 6th February 1958.

[92]   Jeffrey Holland, interview with the author, 2017.

[93]   *The Stage*, 5th September 1957.

[94]   *The Herald*, 1st August 1958.

[95]   *The Stage*, 1st September 1994.

[96]   Peggy Mount, *Desert Island Discs* interview, 1996.

[97]   *The Stage*, 27th March 1958.

[98]   *The Stage*, 28th August 1958.

[99]   *The Birmingham Post & Gazette*, 21st August 1958.

[100] Peggy Mount, *Desert Island Discs* interview, 1996.

[101] *The Stage*, 10th July 1958.

[102] *The Stage*, 5th February 1959.

[103] *Television Today.*

[104] Peggy Mount, *Desert Island Discs* interview, 1996.

[105] *Television Today.*

[106] Peggy Mount, *Desert Island Discs* interview, 1996.

[107] The first four series of *The Larkins* ran September 1958-October 1960 with a further two series November 1963-August 1964.

108 *The Stage*, 16th April 1959.

109 *Daily Herald*, 6th June 1959.

110 *The Stage*, 11th June, 1959.

111 *Margaret Rutherford – Dreadnought with Good Manners* by Andy Merriman, Aurum Press, 2009, pg. 184-85.

112 Damaris Hayman, interview with the author, 2017.

113 Georgina Moon, interview with the author, 2017.

114 *Coventry Evening Telegraph TV Extra*, 16th June 1979.

115 John Holmes, email to the author, 2017.

Chapter 4

116 Peggy Mount, *Desert Island Discs* interview, 1996.

117 Dame Judi Dench, email to the author, 2017.

118 Eira Griffiths, letter to the author, 2017.

119 Sir Tom Courtenay, letter to the author, 2017.

120 *The Stage*, 21st January 1960.

121 Tommy Steele OBE, letter to the author, 2017.

122 *The Illustrated London News*, 19th November 1960.

123 *The Stage*, 25th October 1962.

124 Diana Hoddinott, letter to the author, 2018.

125 Thelma Barlow, letter to the author, 2018.

126 Jack Smethurst, interview with the author, 2017.

127 *The Tatler*, 9th January 1963.

128 *Radio Times Guide to TV Comedy*.

129 Mark Curry, email to the author, 2018.

130 Pam Valentine, interview with the author, 2017.

131 John Standing, interview with the author, 2017.

132 *The Stage*, 16th January 1964.

133 *Daily Mirrror*, 20th March 1964.

134 Mark Curry, email to the author, 2018.

135 Peggy Mount, *Desert Island Discs* interview, 1996.

[136] Peggy Mount, *Desert Island Discs* interview, 1996.

[137] *The Stage*, 17th September 1964.

Chapter 5

[138] *TV Times*, 19-25th November 1966.

[139] Susan James, telephone call to the author, 2017.

[140] *The Stage*, 6th February 1969.

[141] *The Stage*, 24th November 1966.

[142] *The Stage*, 22nd June 1967.

[143] Mark Lester, email to the author, 2018.

[144] Peggy Mount, *Desert Island Discs* interview, 1996.

[145] Eira Griffiths, interview with the author, 2017.

[146] *Coventry Evening Telegraph TV Extra,* 16th June 1979.

[147] Peggy worked with Wayne in *Oh Clarence!* (the John Chapman comedy adapted from stories by P. G. Wodehouse) at the Lyric Theatre, playing Dame Daphne. Jon Pertwee also featured in the cast.

[148] *The Stage*, 28th August 1969.

[149] Duncan C. Weldon/Ann Sidney, email to the author, 2018.

[150] *The Stage*, 7th January 1971.

[151] *The Stage*, 14th January 1971.

[152] *The Birmingham Post*, 19th December 1973.

[153] Jimmy Perry, *A Stupid Boy*, Century, 2002.

[154] *Daily Mirror*, 23rd October 1971.

[155] Hugh Lloyd, *Thank God For A Funny Face*, John Blake, 2002.

[156] Damaris Hayman, interview with the author, 2017.

[157] Ian Masters, interview with the author, 2017.

[158] Further stage work at the time included *The Rivals* (1972) in which Peggy 'alternatively booming like a bittern and cooing like a corncrake impersonating a dove, brought a new dimension to the personality of Mrs Malaprop' (*The Stage*, 9th March 1972).

In 1973 she starred in the world premiere of Colin Morris's *Jack and Knaves* with Geoffrey Hughes and Leslie Schofield at the Palace, Westcliff.

Not all roles were especially enjoyable. Richard Stone, Peggy's long-time theatrical agent, wrote in his memoirs that the role of the grandmother in *There Goes the Bride* was a 'thankless part' for Peggy and went on to say that Bill Pertwee claimed Peggy had a 'hate parade' 'in which Ray Cooney for writing it, Jan Butlin for directing it, Geoffrey Sumner for having a better part and I for getting her the job vied each week for the position of number one!' (Richard Stone, *You Should Have Been in Last Night*, 2000).

[159] Terence Frisby, email to the author, 2017.

[160] *The Birmingham Post*.

[161] Georgina Moon, interview with the author, 2017. George Moon (1909-1981), English character actor and father of actress Georgina Moon, would work with Peggy on both stage and television.

[162] Ray Cooney, OBE, interview with the author, 2017.

[163] Jeffrey Holland, interview with the author, 2017.

[164] Georgina Moon, interview with the author, 2016.

[165] Claudia Mayer, interview with the author, 2018.

[166] Ann Sidney, email to the author, 2018.

[167] *The Stage*, 13th December 1973.

[168] *The Birmingham Post*, 26th June 1975.

[169] *Daily Mirror*, 14th January 1975.

[170] Bill Bryden CBE, email to the author, 2018.

[171] *The Stage*, 4th November 1976.

[172] Bill Bryden, taken from *So Much Love*, Beryl Reid, Hutchinson, 1984.

[173] Ian Talbot, interview with the author, 2017.

[174] *The Stage*, 2nd September 1976.

[175] Mike Grady, email to the author, 2018.

[176] *Born Brilliant – The Life of Kenneth Williams*, by Christopher Stevens, pg. 285.

[177] Source: *The Kenneth Williams Diaries*, Davies, Russell (editor).

[178] Baroness Floella Benjamin, letter to the author, 2018.

[179] *The Birmingham Post*, 5th December 1977.

[180] *The Birmingham Post*, 22nd October 1977.

[181] *The Birmingham Post*, 22nd October 1977.

[182] *The Sunday Telegraph*.

[183] Dame Penelope Wilton, letter to the author, 2017.

[184] *The Stage*, 8th June, 1978.

[185] *The Stage*, 8th June, 1978.

[186] John Standing, interview with the author, 2017.

[187] In the 1978 production of *Blithe Spirit* at the Palace Theatre, Westcliff, she worked alongside Charmian May (as Ruth Condamine) who played Marjorie Milton in *You're Only Young Twice*.

[188] Eira Griffiths, interview with the author, 2017.

[189] *Weekend*, 2nd-8th November, 1977.

[190] *Basildon Canvey Southend Echo*, 8th March 2007.

Chapter 6

[191] Pam Valentine, interview with the author, 2017.

[192] *The Evening Express*, 27th September 1977.

[193] Pam Valentine, interview with the author, 2017.

[194] Pam Valentine, interview with the author, 2017.

[195] Johnny Wade, email to the author, 2017.

[196] Sir Ian McKellen, letter to the author, 2017.

[197] Pam Valentine, interview with the author, 2017.

[198] *The Birmingham Post*, 16th November 1979.

[199] *The Stage*, 20th November 1980.

[200] Norman Eshley, telephone call to the author, 2018.

[201] *The Stage*, 1st October 1981.

[202] Dame Barbara Windsor, telephone call to the author, 2016.

[203] *The Stage*, 11th November 1982.

[204] Ann Sidney, email to the author, 2018.

[205] *Roll Out the Beryl! The Authorised Biography of Beryl Reid*, Kaye Crawford, Fantom Publishing, 2016.

[206] Ayshea Brough, interview with the author, 2017.

[207] Ayshea Brough, interview with the author, 2017.

[208] Niamh Cusack, letter to the author, 2017.

[209] Oliver Ford Davies, letter to the author, 2017.

[210] *The Stage*, 4th October 1984.

[211] *Evening Chronicle*, 29th March 1984.

[212] Georgina Moon, interview with the author, 2017.

[213] J. C. Trewin.

[214] *The Stage*, 1st August 1985.

[215] Ian Talbot, interview with the author, 2017.

[216] Ian Talbot, interview with the author, 2017.

[217] Ian Talbot, interview with the author, 2017.

[218] Claudia Mayer, interview with the author, 2018.

[219] *The Stage*, 23rd January 1986.

[220] Freddie Davies, conversation with the author, 2018.

[221] *The Stage*, 14th January 1988.

[222] Eira Griffiths, letter to the author, 2017.

[223] Pam Valentine, interview with the author, 2017.

[224] Pam Valentine, interview with the author, 2017.

[225] Mark Curry, email to the author, 2018.

[226] Damaris Hayman, interview with the author, 2017.

[227] Pam Valentine, interview with the author, 2017.

[228] Eira Griffiths, interview with the author, 2017.

[229] *Daily Mirror*, 23rd October 1971.

[230] Ian Talbot, interview with the author, 2017.

[231] *Weekend*, 2nd-8th November 1977.

[232] *Coventry Evening Telegraph TV Extra*, 16th June 1979.

[233] Claudia Mayer, interview with the author, 2018.

[234] Pam Valentine, interview with the author, 2017.

[235] Peggy Mount, *Desert Island Discs* interview, 1996.

[236] *The Stage*, 6th April 1989.

[237] Louise Jameson, email to the author, 2018.

[238] Mark Piper, letter to the author, 2018.

[239] Mark Piper, letter to the author, 2018.

Chapter 7

[240] *Daily Mirror*, 23rd October 1971.

[241] Mark Curry, email to the author, 2018.

[242] *The Times*, 14th November 2001.

[243] Gareth Jones, email to the author, 2017.

[244] Pam Valentine, interview with the author, 2017.

[245] David Scott, email to the author, 2018.

[246] Sylvester McCoy, email to the author, 2018.

[247] Georgina Hale, telephone call to the author, 2017.

[248] Christine Lohr, email to the author, 2018.

[249] Private information.

[250] Mark Curry, email to the author 2018.

[251] Philip Draycott, interview with the author, 2017.

[252] Peter Holmes, email to the author, 2018.

[253] Jeffrey Holland, interview with the author, 2017.

[254] *The Stage,* 21st December 1995.

[255] *The Stage,* 6th January 1995.

[256] This was Hazel Bainbridge's final stage appearance – she died in 1998 aged eighty-six.

[257] Jean Fergusson, letter to the author, 2017.

[258] Niall Leonard, email to the author, 2018.

[259] Mark Piper, letter to the author, 2018.

[260] John Standing, interview with the author, 2017.

[261] Taken from Eira Griffiths' eulogy at the funeral of Peggy Mount, 19th November 2001.

[262] Peggy Mount, *Desert Island Discs* interview, 1996.

[263] *Uncle Vanya* at the Albery Theatre (17th September 1996 – 16th November 1996) proved to be Peggy's swansong. Interestingly the play saw Peggy reunited with Alec McCowen (1925-2017), playing a 'forceful invalid', with whom she had worked decades earlier in *Romeo and Juliet*. The even older Constance Cummings CBE (1910-2005) also featured in the production.

[264] *The Stage*, 18th July 1996.

[265] Bill Bryden CBE, email to the author, 2018.

[266] Mark Piper, letter to the author, 2018.

[267] *The Stage*, 19th December 1996.

[268] Nigel Ellacott, email to the author, 2018.

[269] Mark Curry, email to the author, 2018.

[270] *The Independent.*

[271] *The Stage*, 24th December 1997.

[272] Ian Talbot, interview with the author, 2017.

[273] Georgina Moon, interview with the author, 2016.

[274] Eira Griffiths, interview with the author, 2018.

[275] Ian Talbot, interview with the author, 2017.

[276] Eira Griffiths, interview with the author, 2018.

[277] Ian Talbot, interview with the author, 2017.

[278] Mark Curry, email to the author, 2018.

[279] Jeffrey Holland, interview with the author, 2017.

[280] *The Stage*, 7th May 1998.

[281] Eira Griffiths, interview with the author, 2018.

Chapter 8

[282] Nicolas Ridley, *Godfrey's Ghost – From Father to Son*, Mogzilla Life, 2009.

283 Private information.

284 Eira Griffiths, interview with the author, 2017.

285 Eira Griffiths, interview with the author, 2017.

286 Pat Coombs, letter to the author, 2nd September 2000.
     Anthony Steel predeceased both Peggy Mount and Pat Coombs and died on 21st March 2001 at the age of eighty.

287 Ian Talbot, interview with the author, 2017.

288 Pam Valentine, interview with the author, 2017.

289 Ayshea Brough, interview with the author, 2017.

290 Pat Coombs, letter to the author, 26th June 1999.

291 Pat Coombs, letter to the author, 8th August 1999.

292 Zulema Dene, letter to the author, 2017.

293 Eira Griffiths, interview with the author, 2017.

294 Pat Coombs, letter to the author, 29th April 2000.

295 Pat Coombs, letter to the author, 19th June 2000.

296 Penny Hey, email to the author, 2017.

297 Zulema Dene, letter to the author, 2017.

298 Mark Curry, email to the author, 2018.

299 Eira Griffiths, interview with the author, 2017.

300 Eira Griffiths, interview with the author, 2017.

301 Taken from Eira Griffiths' eulogy at the funeral of Peggy Mount, 19th November 2001.

302 *The Guardian*, 14th November 2001.

303 *Telegraph*, 14th November 2001.

304 *The Independent*, 14th November 2001.

305 Ayshea Brough, interview with the author, 2017.

306 Christopher Biggins, letter to Eira (Griffiths) and Harry Darton, 7th January 2002.

307 Bill Bryden CBE, email to the author, 2018.

308 Mark Curry, email to the author, 2018.

309 Pam Valentine, interview with the author, 2017.

310 Taken from Eira Griffiths' eulogy at the funeral of Peggy Mount, 19th November 2001.

311 Eira Griffiths, interview with the author, 2017.

Index

Ackland, Joss CBE (1928-), 57, 134, 180

Ackland, Rodney (1908-1991), 52

Adams, Polly (1939-), 95

Aitchison, Suzy (1960-), 161

Aitken, Maria (1945-), 113

Alan, Ray (1930-2010), 15, 184

Alexander, Terence (1923-2009), 174

Allen, Stuart, 90

Anderson, Dame Judith (1897-1992), 57

Andrews, Dame Julie (1935-), 32

Anne, HRH The Princess Royal (1950-), 98

Arnaz, Desi (1917-1986), 50

Ashcroft, Dame Peggy (1907-1991), 76

Asherson, Renée (1915-2014), 75

Ashley, Cissie, 34, 171

Ashton, Michael, 100, 104–5

Bainbridge, Hazel (1911-1998), 38, 137, 157, 176, 200

Baker, Hylda (1905-1986), 137, 180

Ball, Lucille (1911-1989), 50

Bamberger, Hilary (1936-), 50

Barber, Frances (1957-), 142

Barker, Dennis, 164

Barlow, Thelma (1929-), 61–62

Barnett, Lady Isobel (1918-1980), 62

Barron, Keith (1934-2017), 61

Barry, John, 28

Barrymore, Michael (1952-), 117

Basilico, Rene, 74

Bassey, Dame Shirley (1937-), 32

Bayliss, Jean (1931-), 25, 155

Bayntun, Amelia (1919-1988), 47

Beeny, Christopher (1941-), 117, 177

Bell, Ann (1938-), 60, 65

Benjamin, Baroness Floella OBE (1949-), 92–93

Benjamin, Christopher (1934-), 61

Bennett, Alan (1934-), 15, 129

Bentine, Michael (1922-1996), 48

Best, Gordon James, 89

Biggins, Christopher (1948-), 166

Bloom, Claire CBE (1931-), 134, 180

Bonner, Neil, 137

Booth, Anthony (1931-2017), 84

Bouchier, Chili (1909-1999), 148, 158, 184

Bowers, Lally (1917-1984), 100, 101–2

Bradbury, Ray (1920-2012), 128, 183

Braden, Bernard (1916-1993), 48

Brazier, Philip & Sally, 12, 13, 17–18

Bresslaw, Bernard (1934-1993), 116, 117, 133, 157

Brough, Ayshea (1948-), 4, 29, 111–12, 154, 165–66

Bruce, Brenda OBE (1919-1996), 129

Bruce, Judith, 110

Bryan, Dora OBE (1923-2014), 89, 150

Bryden, Bill CBE (1942-), 90, 108, 142, 143, 166

Burdess, Jean (1925-2002), 38

Burne, Rosamond (1910-1975), 67

Buxton, Judy (1950-), x

Byrne, Patsy (1933-2014), 89

Caine, Marti (1945-1995), 184

Calder, David (1946-), 128

Calvert, Phyllis (1915-2002), 1

Cannon, Esma (1905-1972), 47, 178

Cant, Brian (1933-2017), 175

Cargill, Patrick (1918-1996), 139, 157

Carney, Tom. *See* Penney, Henry

Carr, Jane, 93

Carroll, Belinda (1945-), 137

Carroll, Lewis (1832-1898), 32

Carson, Violet OBE (1898-1983), 62, 165

Cary, Falkland (1897-1989), 37, 46

Cater, John (1932-2009), 113

Chapman, John (1927-2001), 196

Chappell, William, 52

Chetwyn, Robert (1933-), 80, 82, 83

Clary, Julian (1959-), 133, 149, 184

Clay, Nicholas (1946-2000), 89, 132, 133

Clements, Sir John (1910-1988), 76

Codron, Sir Michael (1930-), 80, 82, 83

Coffey, Denise (1936-), 81, 82

Coleman, Richard (1930-2008), 38, 39

Collins, Edward Charles (brother-in-law), 11

Collins, Winifred. *See* Mount, Nancy

Cookman, Anthony, 41

Cookson, Georgina (1918-2011), 176, 179

Coombs, Pat (1926-2002), xi, xiii–xiv, 30, 34, 64, 77, 78, 100, 102–3, 104, 105, 106, 108, 149, 153, 154–55, 155–57, 158–62, 183, 184, 202

Cooney, Ray OBE (1932-), 85–86, 197

Copeland, James (1918-2002), 38

Corbett, Harry H. OBE (1925-1982), 65, 179

Corbett, Ronnie CBE (1930-2016), 49

Cornwall, HRH the Duchess of *aka* Parker Bowles, Camilla (1947-), 159

Corrigan, Nick, 17

Courtenay, Sir Tom (1937-), 59, 130, 176

Couttie, Earl, 38

Couttie, Earle (1922-2005), 38

Craig, Daniel (1968-), 139

Craven, Gemma (1950-), 89

Cribbins, Bernard OBE (1928-), 63, 174

Cummings, Constance CBE (1910-2005), 142, 201

Curry, Mark (1961-), 4, 9, 14, 31, 34–35, 40–41, 42, 63, 66, 119–20, 127, 132, 145–46, 148, 162, 166

Cusack, Niamh (1959-), 113

Dalglish, Darren, 142

Dann, Larry (1941-), 110

Darton, Eira. *See* Griffiths, Eira

Darton, Harry (1929-), x, 4, 32, 33, 119, 120, 141, 145, 149, 152, 163, 168

Davenport, Claire (1933-2002), 75

Davies, Freddie (1937-), 117

Day, Christopher, 144

de Havilland, Dame Olivia (1916-), 14

Dean, Lee, 125

Degas, Brian (1935-), 132

Dench, Dame Judi (1934-), 4, 57, 58–59, 60

Dene, Zulema (1934-), 155, 162

Denham, Maurice OBE (1909-2002), 153

Denison, Michael CBE (1915-1998), 1, 148

Dewhurst, Dorothy (1886-1959), 48

Dickinson, Reverend David, 167

Dighton, John (1909-1989), 113

Diss, Roger, 13, 96–97

Dixon, Jill (1935-), 38

Dodd, Sir Ken (1927-2018), 32, 148

Doidge Ripper, Cecelia (1943-2010), 34

Dolin, Sir Anton (1904-1983), 88

Dotrice, Roy OBE (1923-2017), 107

Douglas, Jack (1927-2008), 158, 176

Downs, Jane (1935-2015), 174

Draper, Peter (1925-2004), 49

Draycott, Philip (1947-), 133

Dresdel, Sonia (1909-1976), 70–71

Driver, Harry (1931-1973), 68

Dunn, Clive OBE (1920-2012), 111, 184

Dunn, Kate, 22, 26

Eaton, Shirley (1937-), 47, 51, 178, 179

Eddington, Paul (1927-1995), 61, 187

Edinburgh, HRH Prince Philip, Duke of (1921-), 98

Edwards, Jimmy (1920-1988), 76, 112, 175

Elgar, Avril (1932-), 52, 66, 179

Elizabeth II, HM Queen (1926-), 93, 98, 141

Ellacott, Nigel, 144

Elliott, Paul (1947-), 84

Emery, Dick (1915-1983), 1

Emney, Fred (1900-1980), 75

Eshley, Norman (1945-), 109

Evans, Michael, 31, 32–33, 168

Evans, Norman (1901-1962), 172

Eve, Trevor (1951-), 142

Faithfull, Marianne (1946-), 88, 174

Farago, Peter, 93–94

Farquhar, Malcolm (1924-), 89

Fergusson, Jean (1944-), 137–38, 155, 156

Fielding, Fenella OBE (1927-2018), xi, 92, 150

Fleeson, Margery (1894-1980), 45

Flitcroft, Debbie, 161

Fogarty, Jan, 21–22

Fontaine, Joan (1917-2013), 14

Ford Davies, Oliver (1939-), 113

Forsyth, Sir Bruce (1928-2017), 61, 62, 173

Franklin, Gretchen (1911-2005), 84

Franklin, Patricia (1942-), 120

Freeman, Jane (1935-2017), 47

French, Dawn (1957-), 135

Frisby, Terence (1932-), 79–84, 175

Fyffe, Patrick (1942-2002), 137

Garner, Rex (1921-2015), 77, 78

Gémes, József (1939-2013), 134, 180

Gillam, Melville, 37

Gilling, John (1910-1984), 36, 178

Gilmore, Peter (1931-2013), 89, 174

Godsell, Vanda (1922-1990), 38

Goodwin, Harold (1917-2004), 183

Gordon, Noele (1919-1985), 24, 172

Gordon, Oliver, 48

Grade, Lew (Lord Grade) (1906-1998), 158

Grady, Mike (1946-), 90, 91

Grainger, Gawn (1937-), 109

Grant, Deborah (1947-), 124

Gray, Dulcie CBE (1915-2011), 148

Grayson, Larry (1923-1995), 184

Green, Sid (1928-1999), 63

Grenfell, Joyce OBE (1910-1979), 165

Griffiths, Eira *aka* Griffiths-Darton, Eira (1927-), x, 13, 15, 31, 33–34, 42, 59, 73, 87, 97, 118, 119, 120–21, 123, 124, 139, 140, 141, 147, 148, 149, 150, 152–53, 154, 156, 158, 163–64, 167–68

Griffiths, Richard OBE (1947-2013), 114

Guinness, Sir Alec (1914-2000), 66–67, 179

Guyler, Deryck (1914-1999), 76, 182

Gyseghem, Andre Van (1906-1979), 37, 39

Hale, Georgina (1943-), 130

Hall, Adelaide (1901-1993), 15

Hall, Willis (1929-2005), 61

Hampton, Christopher CBE (1946-), 91

Hancock, Sheila CBE (1933-), 129

Hancock, Tony (1924-1968), 69

Handl, Irene (1901-1987), 51, 179

Hanson, Harry (1895-1972), 21–22, 34, 171

Hardwick, Paul (1918-1983), 93

Hardy, Oliver (1892-1957), 103

Hare, Doris MBE (1905-2000), 153, 184

Harris, Naomie OBE (1976-), 139

Harrison, Kathleen (1892-1995), 47

Hauptmann, Gerhart (1862-1946), 67

Hawdon, Robin (1939-), 110

Hawtrey, Charles (1914-1988), 51, 179

Hayes, Patricia OBE (1909-1998), 67

Hayman, Damaris (1929-), 29, 30, 53–54, 79, 120

Henson, Basil (1918-1990), 95

Hey, Penny, 30, 159

Hill, Rose (1914-2003), 153

Hills, Dick (1926-1996), 63

Hird, Dame Thora (1911-2003), 47, 62, 129, 178

Hoare, Mr, 9

Hoddinott, Diana (1945-), 61

Holland, Eleanor, 86

Holland, Jeffrey (1946-), x, 30, 34, 44, 86–87, 136, 149
Holmes, John, 13, 56
Holmes, Peter, 136
Hood, Morag (1945-2002), 108
Horrocks, Jane (1964-), 113
Houston, Renée (1902-1980), 92
Howerd, Frankie OBE (1917-1992), 130, 157, 173, 182, 183
Hudd, Roy OBE (1936-), 111, 161
Hulbert, Jack (1892-1978), 84

Inman, John (1935-2007), 158, 187

Jackson, Freda (1907-1990), 75, 94
Jackson, Gordon OBE (1923-1990), 47, 67, 178
Jacobi, Sir Derek (1938-), 142–43, 177
Jacques, Hattie (1922-1980), 62, 92, 121, 165
James, Sid (1913-1976), 68, 69, 70, 166, 182
James, Susan, 70
Jameson, Louise (1951-), 124–25
Jameson, Marion (1924-1983), 124–25
Jefferies, Lionel (1926-2010), 130
Jefford, Barbara OBE (1930-), 57
Johns, Milton (1938-), 61
Jones, Gareth (1951-), 128
Jones, Gemma (1942-), 114
Jones, Griffith (1909-2007), 113

Karen, Anna (1936-), 47
Karlin, Miriam OBE (1925-2011), 23, 66, 94, 179
Kaye, Davy (1916-1998), 63
Keith, Sheila (1920-2004), 153
King, Dave (1929-2002), 48
King, Diana (1918-1986), 100

King, Philip (1904-1979), 37, 46
Kingston, Mark (1934-2011), 130
Kitt, Eartha (1927-2008), 32
Knowles, Michael (1937-), 77
Kossoff, David (1919-2005), 48, 49, 50, 179

La Rue, Danny OBE (1927-2009), 88
Lambda, Peter (d. 1995), 67
Lancaster, Ann (1920-1970), 11
Laurel, Stan (1890-1965), 103
Lawley, Sue (1946-), 8, 16, 187
Le Mesurier, John (1912-1983), 69, 180, 182
Ledger, Peggy (1900-1981), 104
Leigh-Hunt, Barbara (1935-), 60
Leighton, Margaret (1922-1976), 44
Lenska, Rula (1947-), 124
Leonard, Niall (1959-), 138–39
Lester, Mark (1958-), 72, 180
Lewis, Ronald (1928-1982), 47, 178
Lillie, Beatrice (Lady Peel) (1894-1989), 44
Littlewood, Joan (1914-2002), 47
Lloyd, Hugh MBE (1923-2008), 75, 77, 78–79, 175, 183
Lockwood, Margaret CBE (1916-1990), 62
Lockwood, Mrs, 9
Lockwood, Stella, 9
Lodge, David (1922-2003), 148
Lohr, Christine, 130–31
Lollobrigida, Gina (1927-), 67, 179
Lom, Herbert (1917-2012), 44
Lott, Barbara (1920-2002), 49
Lowrie, Philip (1936-), 53

MacDonald, Aimi (1942-), 175
Maggs, Harry & Joan, 12, 18–20
Maggs, James, 18–20
Mantle, Doreen (1926-), 109

March, Elspeth (1911-1999), 156

Marlowe, Anthony, 38

Marner, Richard (1921-2004), 136, 176

Marsden, Betty (1919-1998), 153

Marsh, Keith (1928-2013), 69, 84, 182

Marshall, Zena (1926-2009), 36, 178

Massey, Anna (1937-2011), 187

Massey, Daniel (1933-1998), 114

Masters, Ian, 31, 79, 175

Mathis, Johnny (1935-), 32

May, Charmian (1937-2002), 198

Mayall, Rik (1958-2014), 134, 180

Maynard, Bill (1928-2018), 117

McAlinney, Patrick (1913-1990), 52

McAuliffe, Nicola (1955-), 130

McCarthy, Dennis (1933-1996), 56

McCowen, Alec CBE (1925-2017), 201

McCoy, Sylvester (1943-), 130

McGarry, Peter, 55-56

McKellen, Sir Ian (1939-), 28, 40, 76, 107

McKenzie, Julia (1943-), 187

McNeice, Ian (1950-), 138

Merivale, John (1917-1990), 38

Middlemass, Frank (1919-2006), 89

Millar, Mary (1936-1998), 108

Milligan, Spike KBE (1918-2002), 148

Mills, Sir John (1908-2005), 148

Mitchell, Barbara (1929-1977), 50

Moody, Ron (1924-2015), 66, 179, 180

Moon, George (1909-1981), 85, 197

Moon, Georgina, 55, 85, 87, 102, 114, 147, 154

Moore, William (1916-2000), 23, 75

Moran, Richard, 109

Morgan, Ric (1946-2017), 15

Morley, Robert CBE (1908-1992), 65, 66, 76, 179, 180

Morris, Colin (1916-1996), 88, 197

Morvern, Myrette (1907-1986), 38

Mount, Alfred John (1884-1930) (father), 1-2, 3-4, 4-5, 6, 72, 190

Mount, Alice *née* Covell, 2

Mount, Edward (paternal grandfather), 2

Mount, Nancy (1912-2011) (sister), 2-3, 4, 5, 6, 8, 9, 11-21, 56, 72-73, 106, 120, 165, 168, 191

Mount, Peggy OBE (Margaret Rose Mount) (1915-2001)

amateur dramatics, 8, 21-22, 96

birth (1915), 1, 190

blindness, 88, 126, 139, 142-43, 144-49, 151, 154, 155, 158, 162, 164

cars and driving, 4, 55, 87, 88, 106, 112, 117, 118

childhood injury, 6-7

cooking, 27, 87, 106, 118-19, 119-20, 122, 165

death (2001), xiv, 32, 163-64

death of father (1930), 4-5, 6

death of mother (1968), 72-73, 191

declining health, xiv, 155, 157, 161-63

Denville Hall, xiii-xiv, xv, 147, 151, 152-54, 156, 159, 161, 162, 163, 168

film debut, 36-37, 178

final stage appearances, 141-44

final television appearances, 138-39, 148, 149-50

friendships, xiii, xiv, xv, 5, 9, 13, 14, 16, 30, 31-32, 33-34, 64,

95, 97, 102, 103, 114–15,
120–21, 145, 155
funeral, 166–68
George and the Dragon, 68–71,
121, 133, 145, 155, 166, 182
Harry Hanson company, 21–22,
171
health issues, 45, 121, 133, 140,
154, 155, 156, 157, 161, 162
hobbies, 97, 118, 165
house moves, xv, 63–64, 117,
151
Lollipop Loves Mrs Mole, 76–79,
182
OBE (1996), xv, 141, 164
property burgled, 89
public recognition, 55–56
reaction on becoming a star, 40,
44, 46
relationship with father, 3
relationship with mother, 5–6, 7,
9, 29, 43, 73
relationship with sister, 6, 8, 9,
12–16, 43, 106, 120, 165
romances, 29, 34–35
Sailor, Beware!, 27–28, 37–41,
43–44, 45–48, 54, 63, 80, 83,
84, 93, 110, 124, 143, 167,
172, 174, 178, 181, 187
sexuality, 30
strikes, 75–76
stroke, 156, 158
television debut, 36, 181
The Larkins, 49–51, 57, 68, 76,
181, 194
voice, xv, 27–29, 42, 61, 62, 69,
70, 72, 78, 90, 93, 103, 116,
130, 142, 145, 157, 163, 164
weight, 7, 26–27, 69, 103, 121–
23, 134, 140, 153, 157

work in pantomime (1980s-
1990s), 16, 85, 111–12, 117,
136–37, 144, 146, 175, 176,
177
work with the RSC (1983-85),
112–15, 116, 128, 135, 175,
176
You're Only Young Twice, xiv,
43, 55, 64, 100–108, 119,
121, 155, 159, 182, 198

Mount, Rose *née* Penney (1884-
1968) (mother), 1, 2, 3, 5–6, 7, 9,
29, 72–73, 191
Mount, Sarah Ann *née* Camburn
(paternal grandmother), 2
Mower, Patrick (1938-), 117
Muir, Graeme (1916-1987), 105,
106–7, 119

Nagy, Bill (1921-1973), 49
New, Barbara (1923-2010), 176
Newell, Norman OBE (1919-2004),
31–32, 33, 193
Nichols, Dandy (1907-1986), 66,
179
Nimmo, Derek (1930-1999), 109,
123, 175
Normington, John (1937-2007), 142

O'Callaghan, Richard (1940-), 113
O'Connor, Des (1932-), 176
O'Connor, Tom (1939-), 158
O'Mara, Kate (1939-2014), 137
O'Riordan, Shaun (1927-), 50, 68, 74
O'Shea, Tessie (1913-1995), 46
O'Toole, Peter (1932-2013), 158
Ogilvy, Ian (1943-), 130
Olivier, Laurence (Lord Olivier)
(1907-1989), 58

Owen, Bill MBE (1914-1999), 112, 175

Paddick, Hugh (1915-2000), 51
Page, June, 91
Palmer, Toni (1932-), 80
Parnell, Val (1892-1977), 24
Paul, Betty (1921-2011), 67
Pember, Ron (1934-), 80
Penney, Annie *née* Porley (1858-1910) (maternal grandmother), 2
Penney, Henry *aka* Carney, Tom (1859-1911) (maternal grandfather), 2-3, 190
Perry, Jimmy OBE (1923-2016), 77
Pertwee, Bill MBE (1926-2013), 77, 174, 197
Pertwee, Jon (1919-1996), 66, 133, 179, 196
Pertwee, Michael (1916-1991), 51, 65
Phillips, Leslie CBE (1924-), 51, 179
Piaf, Edith (1915-1963), 1
Piper, Mark, 125-26, 139, 144
Pleasence, Donald OBE (1919-1995), 128, 183
Powell, Vince (1928-2009), 68
Preston, Leonard, 90
Price, Dennis (1915-1973), 51, 179
Priestley, J. B. OM (1894-1984), 74, 75, 84
Pringle, Bryan (1935-2002), 93

Quayle, Sir Anthony (1913-1989), 67

Radd, Ronald (1929-1976), 80
Rastell, Kathy, 97
Ray, Trevor, 95
Reader, Phyllis, 8, 170
Readwin, Tony, 157

Reddin, Jacqui, 110
Redgrave, Vanessa (1937-), 75
Reed, Sir Carol (1906-1976), 71, 180
Reid, Beryl OBE (1919-1996), 89-90, 111, 129, 157, 174
Reid, Mike (1940-2007), 16
Richard, Sir Cliff (1940-), 63, 66, 180
Ridley, Althea *née* Parker (1911-2001), 152
Ridley, Arnold OBE (1896-1984), 152
Ridley, Nicolas, 152
Ripper, Michael (1913-2000), 34
Robertson, Andrew (1941-), 84, 175
Robertson, Harry, 132
Robinson, Cardew (1917-1992), 66, 179
Robinson, Fred, 49
Robson, Dame Flora (1902-1984), 94
Robson, Linda (1958-), 117
Roc, Patricia (1915-2003), 1
Roderick, George (1913-1976), 50
Rogers, Mark, 90
Rutherford, Dame Margaret (1892-1972), 52-54, 124, 165, 172
Ryder, Penny, 7, 114

Salberg, George, 48
Salberg, Reginald (1915-2003), 48
Sands, Leslie (1921-2001), 38
Savory, Gerald (1909-1996), 81
Schofield, Beryl, 5
Scott, David, 129
Secombe, Sir Harry CBE (1921-2001), 71, 157, 180, 182
Sellers, Peter CBE (1925-1980), 51, 179
Shand Gibbs, Sheila (1930-), 38
Shaw, Martin (1945-), 91

Sidney, Ann (1944-), 110–11, 112, 175

Simmons Brothers, The, 176

Sims, Joan (1930-2001), 51, 92, 129, 178, 179

Sinatra, Frank (1915-1998), 1

Sleep, Wayne OBE (1948-), 136, 137, 144, 176, 177

Smethurst, Jack (1932-), 62

Smith, Cyril (1892-1963), 37, 45, 46, 47, 178

Smith, Liz MBE (1921-2016), 129, 187

Smith, Roderick, 90

Speight, Johnny (1920-1998), 148

Spriggs, Elizabeth (1929-2008), 129

Stacey, Neil (1941-), 124

Staff, Kathy (1928-2008), 47

Standing, John (1934-), 30, 64–65, 95–96, 102–3, 140

Stanton, Barry (1940-), 93

Stark, Graham (1922-2013), 148, 180, 182

Steedman, Shirley (1950-), 75

Steel, Anthony (1921-2001), 153, 202

Steele, Tommy OBE (1936-), 57, 60, 76, 182

Stevens, Ronnie (1925-2006), 63

Stevenson, John (1937-), 90

Stevenson, Juliet CBE (1956-), 114

Stevenson, Terence, 124

Stoll, David (1922-2013), 23, 62

Stritten, Cliff, 97

Stritten, Grace, 97

Stubbs, Imogen (1961-), 142

Sugden, Mollie (1922-2009), 23, 134

Swinton, Tilda (1960-), 113

Sykes, Eric CBE (1923-2012), 148, 176, 179

Terry-Thomas (1911-1990), 24, 51, 148, 172, 179

Thatcher, Baroness Margaret (1925-2013), 113

Thaw, John CBE (1942-2002), 114, 134

Thomson, Kim (1960-), 132, 133

Thornton, Frank (1921-2013), 75, 150

Tomasin, Jenny (1938-2012), 124

Tomlinson, David (1917-2000), 65, 173

Trouncer, Ruth (1930-), 50

Tutin, Dame Dorothy (1930-2001), 67

Tynan, Kenneth (1927-1980), 59

Valentine, Pam, 3, 30, 64, 100, 101, 102, 103–6, 107, 118–19, 120, 123, 128, 154, 166

Van Der Burgh, Margot (1935-2008), 49

Vari, John, 52

Vaughan, Norman (1923-2002), 175

Vaughan, Peter (1923-2016), 91, 182

Victor, Charles (1896-1965), 36, 178

Wade, Johnny (1933-), 106–7

Waller, Jack, 38

Walsh, Valerie, 110

Walter-Ellis, Desmond (1914-1994), 84

Walters, Dame Julie (1950-), 135

Wanamaker, Zoë CBE (1949-), 114

Ward, Bill, 49–50, 77

Waterhouse, Keith CBE (1929-2009), 61

Watling, Jack (1923-2001), 67

Watts, Queenie (1923-1980), 11

Wayne, Naunton (1901-1970), 74

Welch, Elisabeth (1904-2003), 153

Weldon, Duncan C. (1941-2019),
    75, 84, 88, 110, 142
Welles, Orson (1915-1985), 1
Wellings, Ron (1936-), 81, 83
Wheeler, Terence (1936-), 91
Whitfield, Dame June (1925-2018),
    150, 161
Whittington, Valerie, 108
Wilde, Oscar (1854-1900), 48
Williams, Kenneth (1926-1988), 91–
    92, 174
Wilton, Ann (1899-1980), 38

Wilton, Dame Penelope (1946-), 95
Windsor, Dame Barbara (1937-),
    110, 150, 175
Wisdom, Sir Norman (1915-2010),
    1, 158
Wise, Ernie OBE (1925-1999), 155
Wood, Duncan (1925-1997), 119
Wood, Jeffrey, 27

Zampi, Mario (1903-1963), 51, 179
Zeffirelli, Franco (1923-), 4, 58, 59